Amazing Korean Trio

AMAZING KOREAN TRIO

Life Stories of Three Korean High School Seniors from the East Coast

Edited by

Hojae Jin

The Hermit Kingdom Press
Highland Park Seoul Bangalore Cebu

Amazing Korean Trio: Life Stories of Three Korean High School Seniors from the East Coast

Copyright ©2009 The Hermit Kingdom Press

Hardcover ISBN13: 978-1-59689-086-2
Paperback ISBN13: 978-1-59689-092-3

Write To Address:
The Hermit Kingdom Press
P. O. Box 1226
Highland Park, NJ 08904-1226
The United States of America

Library of Congress Cataloging-in-Publication Data

Amazing Korean trio : life stories of three Korean high school seniors from the East Coast / edited by Hojae Jin.
    p. cm.
 ISBN 978-1-59689-086-2 (hardcover : alk. paper) -- ISBN 978-1-59689-092-3 (pbk. : alk. paper)
 1. Jin, Hojae, 1992- 2. Kang, Kevin, 1992- 3. Yun, David, 1992- 4. Korean Americans--East (U.S.)--Biography. 5. Korean American teenagers--East (U.S.)--Biography. 6. High school seniors--East (U.S.)--Biography. 7. East (U.S.)--Biography. 8. Oral history--United States. I. Jin, Hojae, 1992-
 E184.K6A39 2009
 973.92092'3957--dc22
                              2009032072

TABLE OF CONTENTS

"Determined for Great Destiny: The Story of My Life"

Hojae Jin

Before beginning with my life, I should begin with a brief family history. As far as I know, both my paternal grandparents had pretty normal lives, although they were not easy, since like everyone else at that time, they had to go through the Korean War (1950-1953) at a very young age. The Korean War, which began because of the difference of ideologies between the North and the South, resulted in the death of 2 million people in total. The war halted when the South and the North agreed to a stalemate in 1953 and drew a line across the Korean peninsula and divided it into two separate countries. My paternal grandfather, Du Chil Jin, and In-Ja Kim met each other at a young age in South Korea, got married and had two boys, my dad being the first child. My dad, Duk-Ki Jin, and his younger brother, Sang-Ho Jin both had stable lives, living in relatively prosperous area in Seoul and going to good colleges and getting good jobs. My maternal grandmother, Jung-Lim Lee grew up in a rich family in southern part of Korea in Dae-gu, which was strategically important and was once the capital of South Korea when Seoul was taken by the North. Her father being a doctor, and the Dae-gu being safe from the bullets of the North, my grandmother was relatively comfortable, even avoiding the ongoing rampage of the war until her father suddenly disappeared and never came back from his work. Even after that sudden disappearance, the wealth accumulated enabled my grandmother to go to a very good college to major in piano and pursue her career as a pianist.

My maternal grandfather's family was in North Korea the moment the Korean War broke out. However, like many other people, his family began a long and hard journey of moving to the South because they supported a democratic, capitalistic society, not a communist one. As the family moved south, however, my maternal grandfather, Woong-Suk Yoon's mother died, and because the father had to go around many different places to make money, my maternal grandfather, being the first son, had to take care of his siblings. However, because he studied so hard, he was accepted into the Seoul National University, the top university in Korea. And these two very different people from different social status met in Seoul, got married, and had two children, my mom, Young-Eun Yoon and my uncle, Ki-Yul Yoon.

And my parents, as a result of their parents' persistent, hard works, enjoyed relatively comfortable lives in Seoul. They actually knew each other from when they were in middle school, because their schools were very close. But they started to know each other in their church. In Korea in the 70s and the 80s, Christianity bloomed and had a golden age. However, many people went to church not only for their spiritual lives. Many young people gathered at church for social and communal purposes, since there were not many chances for young people to meet publicly at that time. Even as my parents went to colleges, their connection did not end. They both went to really good colleges in Seoul. My dad went to Yonsei University, majoring in chemical engineering, while my mom majored in clarinet and went to Sook-Myung University, which was very close to Yonsei University. My parents were able to continue to meet each other regularly, and as they did, they fell in love, and almost right after graduating from their colleges, they got married.

One year after my parents' love-filled wedding, I, Hojae Jin, was born on May 30, 1992, in Shim Hospital, a small hospital owned by my maternal grandfather's friend, at the center of Seoul. By that time, my parents had a small apartment at an outskirt city near Seoul. My dad had a stable job, even being exempted from the mandatory military service because he was chosen as the special researcher at SK Chemical, and his company dealt with chemical engineering. Being the first child of my family, I naturally received much attention and love from all my family members, including my grandparents and uncles. Especially because our family was such a small one compared to other traditional Korean families where there are many siblings, cousins, and nephews, the attention and the expectations imposed on me were great even at my very young age. For example, everyone wanted to see me eating a lot and being very healthy. However, I always troubled my family because I did not eat much. I was always very skinny, yet I was neither weak nor short.

Many people who had only seen me a long time ago are much surprised when they see me these days because I was really skinny when I was very young. When looking back at the old pictures of myself, I, too, notice that I looked noticeably skinny compared to other kids of my age. But because of me not eating much and being skinny, my mom always gave me milk to provide me with the necessary nutrition when I asked her for water. So until I went to kindergarten and drank actual water, I had always thought that "water" was the white liquid that quenches my thirst, although it was actually milk. As a result, I am tall and built right now, being almost 6'1''.

After two years at Suwon, my family moved to another small city near Seoul called Gwacheon. Gwacheon is known as a "good city to live" because it has many big parks, an amusement park, and many other convenient facilities. This city is remembered as my hometown to me because most of my childhood memories come from this small city. In Gwacheon, my family started to stabilize, mature and grow economically. Mom started to help the family financially by teaching clarinet at a nearby academy that had both a kindergarten and a music academy. As I became 5 years old, I started going to that kindergarten where my mom's music academy was located. It was an English kindergarten, meaning half of my lessons were taught by English native speakers from America, Canada, or Australia. My parents were aware of the fact that English was becoming more and more important for me to survive in this global world. This choice of having me go to the English kindergarten proved to be a success in my life, since this early exposure to the English language significantly helped me to develop better English pronunciation than many other Koreans, who have hard time acquiring an authentic English accent at an old age. I am always thankful for this wise choice my parents had made of sending me to the English kindergarten.

As I went through my kindergarten age, I continued to grow in everyway. Although I was still skinny, I was always above most of my friends' heights, and did not suffer any serious illness or diseases. Many teachers liked me and I had a very smooth, happy kindergarten years. In those years, I made many significant friends that still remain as my good friends. Kang-Sik Jo, whom I still consider as my best friend, lived below on the 6th floor of my apartment, and I lived on the 7th floor. Although we fought a lot, we always reconciled and played together on a daily basis. We did many things, playing inside and outside continuously, such as playing hide-and-seek, catch, rollerblading, or making toy cars together until one of our parents started calling our names to eat dinner. As we spent so much time together we also became natural rivals, always competing and pursuing a better position in our own social hierarchy of friends. For example, since getting a good toy car could bring upon respect and popularity among friends, we tried to save coins around our houses to get a better toy car than each other's.

After three years of kindergarten years, I went on to elementary school which was ten minutes away from my apartment by foot. Although my best friend Kang-Sik was not in my first grade class, I made many new friends and adjusted well to the new system in which I had to spend the next six years of my life. Second grade was a very important school year for me for a few reasons. First of all, my teacher, Sung-Ae Oh, turned out to be a wise, understanding woman who led her class with love and passion. The teacher's passion influenced everyone in the class including me, and I still remember the impression I have gotten from the teacher: the one of awe and respect. Also, the second grade classes were to elect a class captain for each class at the beginning of the school year. Being a pretty popular guy, I was dragged into the election by some of my friends regardless of my reluctance. But the moment my name was written on the chalkboard as a candidate, I was suddenly drawn into the race and wanted to become the class captain. So in my election speech, I promised my classmates that I would become a diligent, hard-working class captain who would be willing to help out the classmates and would be ready to serve the class as a representative. As the election began and we began to count the votes, I became continually more and more nervous.

My biggest rival was Hye-Soo Kim, who was a very popular girl. By the time there was only one vote left to be opened, Hye-Soo and I both had seventeen votes. All the attention of the class was focused on the last vote. As I tried to control my breath, Mrs. Oh announced that the last vote was for me. The exhilarating, exciting thrill passed through my body, and I was surrounded by congratulating friends. That joyous experience is the most vivid memory that I have in the second grade.

After becoming the class captain, I gained a reputation as a friendly and hard-working student among my friends. And this incident gave me a confidence boost I needed to adjust fully in elementary school. Starting with the second grade, I continued to become the class captain year after year. The second grade was a very successful year in which I gained the needed confidence. My elementary school years passed by without many incidents, as I had a good relationship with all my friends and was obedient to my parents and did what they wanted me to do including going to after-school academies, called "hakwon." I did many things in Gwacheon such as swimming, ice-skating, art, and basketball, and I was proud that I was living in Gwacheon because not many other cities had the facilities that Gwacheon had to provide the people with all this variety of activities. However, I did not know that my parents were planning to leave Gwacheon for my sake.

From fourth grade, I began to vaguely notice that my parents were spending more time talking privately, while trying to avoid my attention. And one day at the end of my fourth grade, they came into my room when I was doing my math homework and carefully began explaining what they have been doing the past few weeks. They told me that they bought a new apartment in Seoul where education opportunities are much better and competition more vigorous among students. They said that we were going to move as soon as the apartment building was finished. That day, I cried with all my might and tried to change my parents' already made decision because Gwacheon has been my hometown, my home, and my refuge. And I did not want to take the challenge of going to a completely new city, the formidable city of Seoul where I heard many things about the choking competitions and hardcore students who study until twelve o'clock every night, and where I would have to give up my reputable social status which I had worked very hard to achieve and make new friends as a new comer, as an outsider.

Also, I would have to part away from my best friend, Kang-Sik, for the first time. All my memories with Kang-Sik rushed into my mind. Our families once went to Thailand for the summer vacation and the friendship between Kang-Sik and me deepened significantly without us realizing as we did so many things together, riding an elephant together at a local Thailand zoo, swimming, and even singing together at a local café. We had not even thought about parting since we were so close and even considered each other as another family member. It was really hard for me to accept the fact that I was moving, and it was even harder for me to tell my friends, especially Kang-Sik, that I was leaving behind everyone to go to Seoul. Most of the friends first showed disbelief, and then despair. Kang-Sik was agonized and extremely sad. So one day during my fifth grade, I promised that I would come visit Gwacheon a lot, and left my beloved hometown and friends to go to the new, unfamiliar city of Seoul.

The life in the center of Seoul was certainly different from the life in Gwacheon. The region to which my family moved was called "Gang-Nam," meaning the south side of the Han River. It was known for the most competitive environment for students since many rich families are concentrated in that region, and most of them spend excessive amounts of money for their children's education. In that high class, luxurious, yet competitive environment, it was hard for me to find a comfortable and relaxed atmosphere I had so easily found back in Gwacheon. However, I was happy that my apartment was much larger and nicer than the one in Gwacheon, and I adjusted well to the school I went to, quickly making many new friends.

One important incident that made everyone remember me in my new school was the final exam at the end of the fifth grade. It was the first time for everyone to take a final exam in elementary school, so the students knew that this exam would determine not only where each student was located academically, but also one's social status, since one's exam score was very important in every aspect in "Gang-Nam." I was determined to study hard for this exam not just because I wanted to give strong impressions to everyone. My parents promised me that if I do really well on this exam, they would buy me a Playstation 2 as a reward. I had never had a game system before, except for an old computer. I was very excited by this offer. I thought of the Playstation 2 that a friend who came back from America after living there for 2 years had.

I was simply astounded by the advanced graphics and the impact it had on that friend's reputation as a "cool guy." If I do well on this exam, I can engrave strong impressions about me on my new friends, as well as getting something that can even more boost up my social status and reputation among friends. From the day my parents offered this challenge, I started studying for the exam like never before. For the first time in my life, I slept later than 12 a.m. to study the five subjects included in the exam: Science, Math, Korean, English and Social Studies.

A week later, I took the exam in school along with all my friends. The exam took us one whole day and the students were all exhausted by the time all the procedures of the exam were over. After school that day, everyone gathered around each other and stared discussing the exam. Because many people had different answers to many different questions, everyone went home nervous. The next day, the exams were all graded and the students got back their test grades one by one. As my teacher handed back my exam packet, I opened it carefully, as my stomach twisted in nervousness. However, as I continued to check through my scores for each subject, I felt greatly relieved. I only had one or two wrongs on each of the subjects, scoring upper 90's overall. And to everyone's surprise, the teacher announced that I received the highest grade in my class. After school, I left school without a word and rushed home. After failing to open the door for 3 times, I finally succeeded, and announced this exciting news even before taking off my shoes. That evening, my family was heading towards a mall, and my mom was busy picking up phone calls from my friends' moms who were congratulating my results. So this exam was another important incident in my life because I was able to step up from the position of a new comer and an outsider to the top of the social status. So, I realized that although I was from an outskirt city, I can exceed even kids in Seoul if I wanted to. I learned that if I try hard enough, I can do anything, and that I am as capable as any other kid that grew up and was educated in Seoul. In addition, I got the Playstation 2 that all my friends were so jealous of, and the advanced game console made me extremely happy.

Although I was doing extremely well in school, I had a little worry in my English after-school academy, or "hakwon." Because there were so many kids in my hakwon who had stayed in America, Canada, or Australia for a long time, it was hard for me to keep up with them, who had firsthand experiences in an English-speaking culture. My parents knew that although I was getting a good English grade in school, it was not enough to actually speak English fluently. After one exam in which many people did better than me, I was so depressed and enraged that I suggested to my parents that I go to an English-speaking country to learn English. My parents started considering this option, and after a long discussion and consideration, we decided that I would go to Canada near Vancouver for about five months to learn English and experience a different culture.

July 30th, 2004. I left Incheon airport for Canada Vancouver airport to take another adventure of my life. Inside the calm, quiet airplane, I silently cried. Too many thoughts rushed into me at once. The image of my mom crying at the airport kept coming up into my mind like the inflow of the tide. It was just impossible for me to build a sand castle in my mind to block this wave of powerful image of my mom crying. I was never away from my parents for more than a week, and being independent of my parents' care was too new and shocking for me. The idea of being alone in a completely new country, a totally new culture scared me. I was not sure if I could even understand what the people in Canada would say, or if I would be able to survive with new Canadian families that I would live with. I did not think of these shocks that almost blew my mind away until the last moment before I boarded the airplane because I was too excited, preparing for the new adventure, learning English with actual native English speakers and meeting new people, including my relative living in Vancouver. I was like a kid who lighted a match for fun without realizing the danger and the impact it might have, other than providing him with the entertainment; I did not realize the significance that living away from my country would have upon my life other than my intellectual life. The long, sleepless seven hours of flight to Vancouver was a very special experience for me. Finally, I landed on Vancouver airport, my face swollen from crying.

The first word I used to describe Canada was "diversity." Having lived in Korea, a mostly homogeneous country, which prides itself for being such a one, I was astounded by the great diversity Canada had. I actually had never seen a black person except in television shows before I went to Canada. And I was fascinated that the people were actually speaking English. To me, English a forever second language, and I learned it only because everyone else around me was learning it, and my parents emphasized the importance in my future life. However, in

Canada, it was a necessary means of survival, the tool of communication. As I was in the midst of all these new inputs of cultural shocks, my relatives and my guardian, Mr. Choi, were there to escort me. Before going to my first Canadian family with whom I would spend a month before September when school begins, I spend a few days at my relatives' house, touring and sightseeing Vancouver and appreciating the presence of my family at such an unfamiliar, exotic place.

I went to many famous places, such as Stanley Park, where I was amazed by the well-preserved nature and the relaxed atmosphere I longed to experience. I had an adjusting period, trying to overcome the jet lag. I was still in shock from being separated from my parents and my homeland. However, the warm attitudes and the psychological help from my relatives and Mr. Choi gave me extra strength to overcome those obstacles.

After a few days with my relatives, I moved into a Canadian family's house, feeling very nervous again. That family actually was professionally taking care of kids from other countries, who came to study English, like me. I was relieved to find few other Korean kids there. Other than three other Korean kids, there were also a very tall French, Jack, and two Chinese twins, Zhang and Xing, who constantly made fun of each other so everyone else can have a good laugh. Although it was a little awkward at first, I found myself talking to my hosts, Linda and Bob, who were very nice and caring. Their race was Italian, and both were of normal height but very fat. They always had the happy, humorous aura around them that made everyone feel comfortable. Also, it was good for me to have a few other foreign students around me because we were able to share our experiences we had as foreign students which made me realize that I was not the only person who was going through all the cultural shocks and hardships. The host family even provided us with Korean food such as Kimchi, which is fermented, spicy cabbage, and ramen, spicy noodle, alleviating my homesickness. During the one month of stay there, I had a preparation period, going to my guardian's English academy, Choi's Learning Center, daily to hone my English skill and get prepared to go to the school in Canada. I was fascinated by the fact that I was actually able to communicate with Linda and Bob quiet fluently even from the beginning of my stay at their house. We had conversations about many things ranging from the current events around the world to my life back when I was in Korea and how it is different from my life in Canada. It was an amazing feeling because all the money that was put into my English education was for this purpose: being able to communicate with the rest of the world. Although most of the kids there had already left by the time it was my time to leave the place, I managed to get really close to the Korean student who was planning to stay there for a much longer time, as well as the hosts, Linda and Bob. So I had to go through another farewell, and another encounter with a new family and a whole new set of family traditions and rules.

The new family I met was also a Canadian family, living in a small house at a town called Mapleridge. The family consisted of two parents, Rachael and Rob, two kids, Tanner, who was one year younger than me and Alex, who was seven years old, a dog, Bailey, and a cat, Pearl. They were all very friendly and fun to be with. I was especially happy that I had a very good companion, Tanner because he was only one year younger than me, and he had a very bright personality, always sharing things with me and welcoming embracing me as a family member. Thanks to this friendly environment, I was quickly absorbed into the family.

As soon as I was settled, however, the school year began, and I had to go to a small public school called Hammond that was about three minutes walk away from the house I was staying. The first day of school was so nerve breaking. I did not know anyone because Tanner went to another school near Hammond, and it was my first time experiencing a school system of another culture. I tried so hard not to look nervous and kept thinking about all the preparations I have made in Korea and Mr. Choi's academy made for me to have a successful semester at Hammond.

I walked straight into the school building, expecting something to happen. However, no one was there. I stood at the entrance for a minute, panicking and thinking really quickly about what to do. But after a few seconds, I saw a few students walking to some other part of the building. Having no choice, I silently followed them and was led to a gym full of students. Feeling quiet awkward among all the students I did not know, once again I stood there quietly and wanted something to happen to eliminate my awkwardness. Few minutes later, to my greatest shock, a man in a clown costume came up to the stage at the front of the gym and introduced himself as the principal of the school. Then he started leading the whole school with dancing and stretching with a loud music. This was unimaginable in Korea. I really wanted this to stop, feeling much more awkward than just standing still in a gym full of people I did not know. Being pretty tall, I noticed that I was very visible, and that many kids were eyeing me. So I had to follow the principal like everybody else and dance and stretch, my whole body burning and sweating in embarrassment.

After about ten minutes of dancing, the music stopped and teachers started calling out for each grade to come gather. One short, old woman with white hair announced that she was responsible for the new comers that day, so I followed her with a few other kids to a small room. There, the woman, who introduced herself as Mrs. Baker explained the basic rules and the system of the school. Students are to report to their classes at eight o'clock, they are to bring their own lunch and eat at the cafeteria and may play at the playground until the end of the recess. Then Mrs. Baker guided us through the school and gave us the general sense of where the important rooms were in the small school building. Then, she informed each of the students whom his teacher was. I was told that my teacher was Mr. Tyler.

Because my guardian had already contacted the school and explained my situation, the school put me in the ESL class, which stands for English as Second Language class. Twice in a week, I received special lessons in basic English skills to enhance my English. After Mrs. Baker dismissed the new students, I had to go to Mr. Tyler's room alone to say hi, when all the students had already gone home. It took me a while to take the courage to knock the closed door of Mr. Tyler's room. I stood there thinking about what I should say and quickly converting those Korean words into English as my hands became cold with nervousness. However, as soon as I knocked, a warm voice from the inside told me to enter. As I gingerly entered the room, I met a middle aged man who seemed to have a very healthy, balanced body despite his graying hair. Mr. Tyler welcomed me heartily, showing great interest in my situation and respect for my decision to come to Canada alone to learn English. I knew that I met a great teacher the moment I saw Mr. Tyler. His disarming attitude and caring voice washed away my awkwardness and nervousness. I was able to talk about him for a while and share many things about me and learn what I was going to be taught this semester generally. In contrast to that morning, I was feeling relieved and joyful as I walked back home.

So my semester in Hammond of Mapleridge began. With the help of Mr. Tyler, I was able to make many new friends within days. My closest friend was Shamus, who was even taller than me, even though I was considered very tall in my class both in Korea and Canada. Shamus approached me first during recess period in which I was expecting to have the most awkward time because everyone had their freedom to do whatever they wanted to do, not just sitting in a classroom and listening to the teacher. Shamus was very amicable and was very curious about my situation and how I came to Canada. So by telling him about my story and listening to his own life story, we became very close friends within first few days of the semester. From there, Shamus introduced me to many other friends including T.J., Ryan, and Nick, who also became my close friends.

Studying was relatively easy because the Canadian education system did not require as rigorous academic requirements as the Korean one did. I excelled in math because I learned everything in Korea that the Canadian students were learning at that time. And because I tried and studied very hard, I did extremely well on all other subjects, too, including French, Social Studies, Science, and English. Instead of teaching from the written textbooks, Mr. Tyler himself made his own textbooks for students and focused on respecting everyone's individuality and creative minds. In one instance, we had this big project in which each student was to make his own ending to a long chronology that Mr. Tyler himself had created about an ape and how he would have survived through the hardships he had to encounter. And there was no limit to the ways in which students could do to make this ending. T.J. made a script and performed in front of the class, while Nick drew a 4 pages long comic. At the end, everyone had a great time comparing each other's ending and discussing whose ending was the best. There, I realized that although many Korean students might have more knowledge, they might not be able to create new things or adjust to new things because the education system in Korea does not allow the students to be creative.

As a result of this loose education system of Canada, I was allowed to do many things I was not able to do in Korea as a student. I played volleyball in a school team, spent time outside with my friends, playing soccer, basketball and catch. I was able to read many books I wanted to read, having lots of free time after studying for one or two hours each day. I was really happy and relaxed as I became used to the school and made many friends with whom I became really comfortable. Especially because I played volleyball well in the school team, many more friends started liking me and I had no trouble making friends. Although I always missed my family and my friends, I did like Canada a lot. Compared to Seoul, people were much more relaxed and the students had much more time to do what they wanted, whatever it was.

5:00 p.m., December 17, 2004. I was busy packing my stuff in my room after having my last day of school in Canada when a group of my friends and the host family rushed into my room and started saying "Good-bye, Nate (which was my English name)" and "We'll miss you a lot" and hugging me. The figures of my loving friends and my host family became blurry as tears started forming in my eyes. After having this small but moving party, I had to go through another farewell with the people I became so close with. All the good times we had together went through my mind as I continuously wiped out my tears. The movies we watched together at the local movie theater, the dragon ball video game in which I played so well that my friends refused to play, all the jokes and pranks we played on each other. They were all about to become another memory.

Finally, Mr. Choi came to pick me up, and I had to make an empty promise that I would visit Mapleridge in a short time and left the house in tears. However, as I boarded the airplane to my homeland, I was again excited about seeing my family and friends again. For the nine hours of flight, my imagination already brought me back to

Korea, seeing all the loved ones once again and sharing the amazing things I have experienced in Canada. Things went just like I imagined during the flight. My parents came running to me and hugged me, and we were all surprised that I grew even taller than my dad now. My grandparents, who also came to the airport, started commenting about my courage and the good work I have achieved in Canada. And as a surprise gift, they bought me an mp3 player that had many Christmas carol songs and popular pop songs. This day is to be remembered by me as one of my happiest days.

Looking back, I think my stay in Canada left many important imprints in my life. Firs of all, since I was away from my parents, the people I relied on the most throughout my life, I grew to be independent. Although I always had people caring for me, such as Linda and Bob, and Rachael and Rob, they were foreigners for me, and I was a foreigner to them. We were always polite to each other and sometimes very intimate, but I had to develop my own skills to be independent, instead of relying upon my host families for the little things I had to do. I remember the first week of my stay in Canada when I had to cut my nails on my own for the first time. Although it was hard, I felt good about myself after I did it because I felt that I was being independent from all the help and caring I have been getting, especially since I am the only child.

Secondly, I developed a skill of making new friends and adjusting to a new system. I was a total foreigner, and I had to give a good first impression not just for myself, but for my country, Korea, because I was a representative of Korea in many people's perspective. So I tried to keep a smile on my face when I met people, and that worked very fine since most people reacted with a smile on their own, and from there, a good relationship was generated. Also, I realized that as well as keeping a smile on my face, being polite would always help me to adjust to a new system whether the system was my new elementary school in Korea or the middle school in Canada.

Thirdly, my stay in Canada brought me a new perspective of the world. Before I went to Canada, Seoul and Gwacheon was the whole world to me. All my mind processes and thoughts were based in that small region in Korea. However, the diversity of ethnic, religious groups and the new cultural and environmental setting have enlightened the locked door of my perspective of the world and opened it widely.

Lastly, through the stay in Canada, my English had improved significantly, and most importantly, the stay had given me a boost of confidence. The vague intimidation that the English language had been impending on me disappeared. The mere fact that I was able to communicate with the native English speakers fluently raised my confidence level. I used to stutter a little when I first came, but that has lessened as well. And as I had to use English to write essays and stories, my grammar, which was my weak point in Korea, also became better.

The weeks following my return to Korea were very joyful for me. It was very strange to see how almost everything remained the same, while I experienced such a different, dynamic world as well as changes in my appearance and the perspective of the world. And yet, I was relieved to see that the things were not changed in Korea. I did not have to make new friends, adjust myself to a completely new world, or try to live with complete strangers. It was as if I had a really long, realistic dream and woke up.

I expected my friends and me to be a little awkward for a while because I had not seen them for months. However, I was very wrong because there was no awkwardness at all, but rather an extreme happiness for seeing each other. And because we were about to graduate from the elementary school in February, we were very relaxed and had very much free time. We used to play soccer for hours in the snow until our sweat and body heat lost their capacity to keep our bodies warm. Then we would go into a convenient store to eat instant ramen, hot and spicy noodle Koreans love. Or, we would go to a PC room, where there are many computers in a room, and play computer games together as a team. These heaven-like days passed by quickly, and our graduation day came.

The graduation took place in the school's auditorium on February 18, 2005. The students sat down on the chairs and listened to the principal's last message to his students while parents were busy taking pictures and trying to find their children. My maternal grandparents came along with my parents and handed me a bunch of flowers as soon as the ceremony was over. My friends and I gathered for the last time, since we were all going to different middle schools. Because we had been so close for the last few months, we did not realize or want to think that this was our last time to be together. After taking a picture and sharing a brief farewell, we all parted, telling each other to break a leg in middle school.

So the time came for me to get ready to go to middle school. In Korea, there is about a 3 weeks long spring break before school semester begins. So after the graduation, the new middle schoolers get busy with preparing themselves for the middle school. My middle school was called Seo-Il Middle School, which was located 10 minutes away from my apartment by foot. I started to resume my life as a student, going to math, English, and Korean hakwons. It was not easy going to academically rigorous hakwons after practically playing and resting for more than half a year. However, because I was well-rested mentally, I was ready to absorb everything I learned very quickly.

As my entrance to middle school approached, my mom and I were about to buy my new uniform for the middle school. Inside the uniform store, we were busy picking the right size for me when mom got a phone call from dad. After talking to dad for a long time, mom hung up and told me that we were going to the United States to stay for at least three years. We are leaving in two months. At first, I did not believe her. It had been only a few months since I had come back from Canada, and I was enjoying my "normal" life in Korea and was excited to go to middle school. I did not want any more radical changes in my life. Although my experience in Canada was very helpful and fun, I was content with the fact that it was a one-time experience. But now mom was telling me that because dad's company decided to send my dad to the United States, I had to give up my normal life in Korea and the rest of the family and friends to face yet another great change in life. Mom and I walked out of the store without buying anything and went home to calm ourselves down. By the time we came home, I was already crying, and a whole box of Kleenex was used to wipe my tears. However, I had to stop crying when I absent-mindedly flushed down the whole mass of Kleenex and the toilet got stuck.

When most of the people heard of our news, they all congratulated us for having such a great opportunity especially for me to be educated in America and even possibly going to a good college in America which many Korean students do not even dare to try. And it would be just great for the whole family to escape crowded Korea to experience a much broader World. Although these words did not lessen my fear and pain of having to leave my country again to the new world, I had to agree that this opportunity was something that many people would desire to have.

This unexpected and unwanted (for me) news brought abrupt changes to the whole family. A few days after the news, my mom brought me used uniforms that she bought for about 2 dollars. She said that since I was only going to attend the middle school for about a month, I would not have to wear a new uniform. Dad had to leave in a month to get a house and basic necessities in America before mom and I would go. And since all our furniture and electronic devices take a month to be shipped to America, we had to start packing and get ready to move. So dad went to America shortly afterwards, and mom and I moved into maternal grandparents' house because we had nothing left in our apartment. My middle school started, and my grandfather had to drive me for 20 minutes each morning to school. The month of my middle school life in Korea was very turbulent because I had no reason to study or try hard to get grades since I was moving to America, and I had a hard time making friends because many of the students in my class, who were already aware of the fact that I was moving, were partly jealous and felt no obligation to spend their time and energy to be friends with a person who was to leave in a few weeks.

After a month, mom and I took careful steps out of my grandparents' house to take another great challenge of leaving our own country and being a foreigner in another country. This challenge was especially hard for my mom just like it was for me when I went to Canada because it was her first time being parted from her parents and her country for a long time, and she was afraid of the language and cultural barrier that would make her powerless, surrounded by whites and blacks she has never seen before. It was hard for me to see mom crying in front of her parents and throughout the most of the flight because I understood how she felt and knew how much it hurt.

After the flight that felt like an eternity, mom and I landed at the JFK airport. Dad was waiting for us, and we were particularly relieved to see him because we were both feeling extremely insecure in this new country. It was apparent that mom was experiencing a similar shock that I had on my first day in Canada. Mom's eyes expanded as she observed a 6 foot 5 African American who broke into tears as he met his parents. She seemed confused because she could not understand what people were saying around her. I felt that mom was greatly discouraged because she realized that she was no longer able to bargain with vendors like she used to do in Korea.

Dad brought us to our new home in a small town, called Harrington Park in Bergen County, New Jersey. Dad chose a house in Harrington Park because it was close to his office which was located in a nearby town called Fort Lee. On our way to our new house, mom kept complaining as we left New York City to move into the Garden State and began to penetrate into a more rural area. Harrington Park, like its name implies, is a town surrounded by a very well-preserved nature. Having lived in only metropolitan area for her entire life, mom was again shocked that she had to live in the middle of a forest. However, our house was very big compared to our apartment in Seoul. It was a two-story house with a front yard, a back yard, a basement, and a nice deck.

The few days after our arrival were particularly hard, both physically and mentally. We had to unpack and arrange our arrived furniture, clean the entire house, and fight the painful jetlag. Furthermore, the feeling of isolation imposed a heavy mental damage on all of the family as the area was not densely populated and we knew no neighbors. Although there was only about a month of school year left, I had to go to school as a 7th grader. Harrington Park Public School had the kindergarten, the elementary school, and the middle school all together in the same building which was relatively newly built and very clean. Although the school had mostly white students, there were about 10 or so Korean kids in my grade, which became a great relieving factor for me. I was once again put into an ESL class which prevented me from taking a Spanish class. It was harder for me to make friends in Harrington Park because unlike in Canada, the students were familiar with Asians, and they were not as fascinated or interested by the new presence of another tall Korean kid as Canadian students had been. As a result, there were less people who approached me first and I had to approach Americans actively to make friends, which was not an easy process. I joined the band in a way to make to more friends. And because I played the clarinet, which my mom had taught me for a long time back in Korea, I was able to blend into the band quiet easily and quickly made a few friends there. I was really thankful that I was able to play the clarinet, because unlike the Korean students in Korea, a lot of American students seemed to be more well-rounded and knew how to play many musical instruments or play sports.

I continued to be in the band in the 8th grade and joined the orchestra in my freshman year of high school. Just as I was about to start making more friends throughout the school, however, the school year ended and the long summer break began.

It was my first summer in America, and neither my parents nor I myself knew what to do with all that time that was given to me. In Korea, I used to go to hakwons and stay there for a significant amount of time each day, just like every other kids around me. However, in America, I could not find a hakwon that would keep me there for a long time. As a result, I decided to buy some English grammar books to study by myself, and went to the near local library to burrow many books to read. Because I had so much time left even after I thought I had studied and read a lot, I begged my parents to buy me a basketball hoop. Dad and I bought and built a basketball hoop the next day, and we were very proud of our perfect job.

That summer, my life was a repeated pattern of the same schedule everyday: eating breakfast, studying and reading, eating lunch, playing basketball, eating dinner, and watching television. Although it might seem boring, I personally enjoyed the summer a lot because I thought my summer in America was much better than practically living in the hakwons like I had in Korea. Moreover, that summer, I finally exceeded my dad's height and lost a lot of weight I had gained throughout the exercise-less years in Korea.

From the summer, I started attending a Saturday Korean school. It was a school that taught the same curricula Korean students were learning in Korea to the Korean students in America. Because my dad's expected term of staying in America was about three years, my parents and I thought that it was important for me to continue my education as a Korean student because it was highly probable that I was going back to Korea in a few years. Every Saturday, even when the actual school began, when most of my friends did what they wanted to do, I had to go to the Korean school and basically have a six days school week. Sometimes I complained because I did not want to wake up early on Saturdays and wanted to just play with my friends. But now I am thankful that I went to Korean school because I now know that through that one extra school day per week of my life, my Korean is still in a great shape, and I am familiar with the Korean education curriculum which can help me greatly in the future when I am with other Koreans.

After the long summer break, my 8th grade began in September. The 8th grade was generally very fun because whether I wanted or not, I was the graduating class once again, and there were many events for the 8th graders. The 8th grade is very important because the grades students get in the year determine the classes they take in high school. For example, students who do well in their history class in 8th grade would advance to history honors class in their high school freshman year. However, I was influenced by the much excited and happy mood of my friends.

Throughout the year, as I made many friends and became used to the American education system once again, I started hanging out with friends and did not pay as much attention to studying as I should have. And as graduation approached, there was a big school play called "Once on this Island" in which almost everyone in the 8th grade participated. Even though I had a minor role in the play, nevertheless I had to spend a lot of time practicing with the rest of the 8th graders, and because I did not know how to manage my time well, my school grade did not come out as well as I had wanted, especially in history and English, with which I was not as comfortable as I was with sciences and math. However, my English skills improved enough to get out of the ESL class by the end of the year.

The graduation and the events prior to the graduation of Harrington Park middle school was much more grand, organized, and exciting than the elementary school graduation I had, a year ago in Korea. First of all, prior to the graduation, the 8th graders went on a class trip to Philadelphia. It was the first time for me to go on a trip that lasted a few days. It was very exciting, sleeping only 3 hours because we were having so much fun just chatting and playing card games. Also, I thought it was very useful for us to go to Philadelphia because that year we were learning the American history, and there were many historically important artifacts in Philadelphia, such as the Liberty Bell.

Moreover, the school play that involved almost every 8th grader was very effective in making many good memories for the students because all of us had to spend a lot of time together almost everyday for more than two months to carefully coordinate and organize everything. When the two nights shows were over successfully, we all hugged each other, unable to say anything. I was both sad and happy that the play was over. Although it was not easy having to attend daily practices and doing the same moves over and over again, the memories and the good times I had with my friends flooded back into my mind, and I was able to tell that everyone else was feeling the same way. Furthermore, there was the big graduation party at a luxurious party house right before the graduation, and it was my first time attending such an elaborate and big party where everyone had to wear formal suits but later turned into a loud dance party with a hired DJ.

The graduation itself was also very impressive. The students all took graduation pictures and had the ceremony in front of all of their families. Each of us received the graduation document from the principal, and together, sang the song 'For Good'. Everyone wished everyone else good luck, hugged each other, and signed each other's year book. I was especially sad because my family was moving again, to a nearby town, called Tenafly, during the summer break. That meant that I would not go to the same high school as most of my friends. We were moving again because we had some disputes with our house owner, and Tenafly High School had the better reputation, and was ranked almost 1st or 2nd among all New Jersey public schools. Since there was a decent house available really close to Tenafly High School at a decent price, we decided to move again. Although I had been in Harrington Park only for about a year, I had so many good memories with the friends there, and I was in despair, yet again, I had to make new friends and adjust to a new school district and a new town.

In July, my family moved to Tenafly. Since the education was one of the priorities for our family, I visited Tenafly High School to choose my courses for the freshman year and get to know the school before I actually started attending it. Although I had already passed the ESL test in Harrington Park and was not required to be in ESL classes anymore, because I had come to America about a year ago, I had to take another ESL test at Tenafly. However, I easily passed it, and my impressed guidance counselor gave me an opportunity to take the highest level courses that a freshman can take. I knew it would not be easy, but I decided to take the challenge.

From the summer before my freshman year in high school, I began to go to an academy that taught the SAT. But because I felt that I had plenty of time before the SAT, I slacked off and basically had a fun time playing with my new friends that I made in the academy. I was able to get to know a few people from Tenafly High School from that academy.

When the school year began in September, I was surprised by the vigorous academic efforts each course required from the students. It was totally different from the middle school's requirements, and I was neither physically nor mentally ready for the surprisingly competitive and hard courses and the amount of work they threw at me, each night.

And during these days I developed a bad habit of always sitting in front of my computer even when I was doing homework, constantly chatting online with my friends, under the justification that I was asking questions about some homework assignments. However, this bad habit harmed me academically more than it helped. Chatting online took a lot of time away from me, and it also distracted me a lot, hindering me from concentrating when I needed to. Although I had a successful freshman year in terms of making many friends and adjusting well to a new school, my academic achievements were not as great. I was not mature enough yet to manage or control my time well.

The World History East Honors class was especially hard for me. The course was already notorious for being a very challenging course with a load of work, and since I was not used to reading long, boring text books in English, I had a hard time understanding exactly what happened 3,000 years ago in India. In the first semester, I received a solid B in that course, and as a result, I was not able to take the 'Humanities' course for the following year, which was a honors course combining English and history. My self-confidence was broken, and I was secretly humiliated by the fact that I was not able to get into that course which I wanted to take. This caused me to study extra hard in my sophomore year in my regular history and

English classes. My freshman year had ended in a disappointment academically.

I started doing community service work from the freshman year in an organization called "Mil Al" which means wheat berry in Korean. It is a Christian organization that helps many mentally disabled people around the world, and I went to one branch of this organization every Friday. At first, I went there because my friend David did not want to go alone. But as we spent our weeks after weeks, we were both very involved in this program, being very proud of the work we did. As I met my friends at Mil Al every week, I realized that I had had a deep prejudice against mentally disabled people even when I did not know any of them personally. I had unconsciously considered mentally challenged people as people who are totally "different" from the rest of us, almost like aliens from the outer space. However, my long journey with them dragged me from this deep swamp of prejudice. I did note that they were different from us, but they were nevertheless the same with us in that they felt emotions and reacted to the people around them the same way they were treated. And they wanted much love and attention from us.

David and I, along with a few other volunteers, tried to be very caring and loving, because we wanted to show that God created everyone equally, and that some people just needed more love and compassion in this world. This program became a part of me and shaped me as a person who learned to care about the others, not just me as an individual. I am still participating in this program once a week, and have recently received the Presidential Award from the White House for my "devotional caring."

Although I felt that it was everyone's obligation to be caring for others, I was still very glad that my weekly volunteer work that became a part of my life brought me this exceptional award.

During the summer break, my family went to Korea because dad's company offered us free airplane tickets after we stayed in America for two years. I was very happy to be in Korea. It was nice to see the family once again, and I was able to see my old friends briefly even though they were all busy with their hakwon schedules. It was very strange to be in Korea and being different from the rest of the students because I was a 'student from America.' Since the schools in Korea begin their summer break in mid-July, I saw myself surrounded by students walking with their uniforms on, while I was wearing normal clothing when I was on my way to the hakwon. I was preparing for the TOEFL test in Korea, which is a standardized English proficiency test that many Korean colleges require from students.

The TOEFL consists of four parts: reading, listening, speaking, and writing. Each part has 30 maximum points, so total of 120 points. Because I was supposed to come back to Korea after a year or two, I needed to do well on this TOEFL test. So I went to the hakwon to prepare for this test. However, I was placed in a special class with other students from all across America, separated from the rest of the students attending schools in Korea. I felt bad because a lot of "normal students" were jealous of my class because most of them thought that the students in America were much happier and fortunate than the students in Korea. In their opinion, students in America had much more opportunity to go to good colleges with less studying and efforts. I can agree that the students in America spend less time studying, but we are more independent and do more creative, various works than the Korean students who concentrate on only studying at hakwons, studying because they are told to do so by their parents and their teachers. American students are more open-minded and study out of their will, not because their parents or teachers force them to do so.

After about two months of stay in Korea, my family came back to America unwillingly since we had so much fun in Korea. I watched many movies with the friends who also went back to Korea for a break from America, and we hung out in cool malls, licking delicious ice cream. Mom also had a lot of fun meeting up with her old friends and going shopping almost daily. When my family was boarding the airplane going back to America, mom joked about how she was like a fish leaving her "water again, and going to the dry land."

On our way, though, we visited Canada for about a week to see our relatives. I was very glad to see the relatives I saw when I first went to Canada, now with my family. They were fascinated about how much I had grown, compared to the last time they saw me, and we had a great time touring and sightseeing Vancouver and its region. This precious time reminded me of the life I had lived in Canada, the life in which I really tried hard to get good grades in school and managed my time well according to my daily schedule even though I was younger. I regretted my irresponsible, poorly managed freshman year, and promised myself that I would do better in the sophomore year.

My family came back to Tenafly, and in two weeks, my 2nd year in high school started. That year, I was determined to get good grades no matter what, so I could get into as many AP courses possible for the following year, so that I could redeem myself from the humiliation I had given myself in the freshman year. I barely touched the computer, unless I really needed to use it for work, and studied very hard every night to prepare for the history and English pop quizzes that no one knew when they would pop up, except for the teachers. As a result, I got A's in both history and English, and I was able to advance into AP English and AP U.S. history the following year, instead of staying in the regular class like the most of the other students in my regular classes.

The sophomore year was generally auspicious, academic-wise. I gained back the confidence and was able to pump up my grade a lot compared to the freshman year. However, as our stay in America exceeded two years, I had anxieties about going back to Korea. Usually, the companies in Korea that send their employees to foreign countries call them back after three years. So while studying for my school courses, I always had to keep in mind that I would have to go back to Korea.

I started getting tutored in Korean and Korean math that had a whole different level from the math that I was learning in the American school. It was not easy doing two different studies at once, but it kept me busy the whole year, and that actually led me to be more efficient and productive. Also, I was proud to be done with the TOEFL. Since Korean colleges had such high standards for acceptable TOEFL score as a "good score", I had to take it three times to get the score I wanted. I got 117 out of 120 which is considered a very good score. I felt as if one big burden was lifted up from my shoulder.

Although my dad used to tell me that we were going back to Korea for sure, I never gave up on my American school grades because I knew that this hard working would pay off in the end in some ways. Korean colleges also do see my high school transcript in America to evaluate me. Also, it would be a great advantage for me if I did well on the SAT's because if I did go back to Korea, I would be able to apply to colleges without having to go through the same process as the normal Korean students. Because I was a special case, staying in America for about three years or more, I could send in my SAT scores, the TOEFL score, and my high school transcript to apply to colleges, not having to take the college entrance test that every Korean student should take.

As a result, I started to really study hard for the SAT's during the summer before my junior year. This summer was my busiest summer because along with studying for the SAT's at a hakwon, five days a week, I had to do an excessive amount of summer homework I had received from the AP courses I was about to take in junior year. Each AP course teacher for chemistry, English, and history gave a lot of homework before the summer break because the courses at Tenafly were very rigorous and the courses have to end before May, when there are AP exams. The history homework was especially long and laborious because the AP U.S. history course at Tenafly was to be finished in one year, while for many other schools, this course was a two-years course, starting with a US history 1 sequence. To compensate for this fact, my history teacher basically gave the students two text books, and we had to read almost half of the books during the summer and do questions in the workbooks. So I had to work very hard throughout the whole summer, but I could not complain because the junior year, or the hardest year before the college, was waiting for me.

The junior year. The idea itself makes a lot of prospective junior students frown and shiver. It is certainly not the best year to have fun and enjoy unless one miraculously has a hobby of studying. The junior year was the hardest year for me also. There was a history test every two weeks throughout the whole first semester, and often it coincided with a chemistry test or an English reading quiz. I had to buy a box of redbull to keep me awake at sleepless nights, and in school, I drank coffee to prevent me from falling asleep during classes. The junior year seemed like an endless journey that would continue forever and eventually kill me when redbull or coffee would not work anymore and all my energy would be drained.

Not only did those AP classes make me suffer, the Korean language and Korean math tutors were rushing me through a load of work as my parents predicted that the company might call us back to Korea by the end of the year 2008. Although I was done with the TOEFL, I still had to take the reasoning SAT and SAT II's to have standardized records on my transcript even if I go back to Korea. All those things combined to overwhelm me each night when I came back from school. Although I took the reasoning SAT twice, my score were not as good as I had hoped them to be, and the all the work started to really impend a huge physical and mental burden on me. To be honest, my biggest stimulus that acted like a battery for me was my girl friend I have known since middle school when I went to a Korean school with her.

Although she was a sophomore, she was very smart, and I pushed myself to be as smart as she, and I did not want to show my weakness by giving up anything that was given to me. Every night when I had to study all night, I thought of my girl friend and that kept me awake and gave me endless power to study very hard. In December of 2008, my parents and I became very sensitive since dad's company could call us at any minute and tell us to come back. We would have to go back to Korea in a month. I was afraid to tell any of my friends or my girl friend because I had a slight hope that something might happen and the company might not call us back. And if I do tell my parents prior to my company's call, it was obvious I would be distracting my friends from studying, making many people very emotional. So my parents and I waited silently for days and days, holding our breaths whenever dad's cell phone rang.

On December 22, 2008, my dad's cell phone finally rang. Dad gave us a nod before he picked up the phone. Although we were all mentally preparing ourselves for going back to Korea, I could not stop but collapse on the sofa and wait for my dad to finish the phone call. Dad slowly hung up and in disbelief, declared that we were to stay one year longer as a result of some internal changes that were happening inside his company. That meant I could graduate from my high school in America, and I could go to a college in America because my parents always half jokingly told me that if we were to stay longer, they would let me go to a college in America. So many emotions went through my head in that split second. I was glad that I could stay with my friends and my girl friend, while that meant that all the work that I have done, preparing to go back to Korea, was for nothing. And although I did really work hard in school, my basic thoughts on my future was always based on Korea and Korean colleges. Now I would have to shift my mind and interest to American colleges. I had a really hard time sleeping that night.

From the next day, I quit all the tutors involving Korean education, and started preparing to go to an American college. I started studying for the SAT II math IIC and chemistry, as well as the AP exams and the reasoning SAT.

From January 2009 to June 2009, I do not remember any specific event that happened to me. I only vaguely remember the hard work and sleepless nights that streaked for many consecutive days. Because now I did not have to worry about studying for Korean subjects, I was more focused on one side of the spectrum. My greatest supports came from my parents and my girl friend, and I was so thankful that I was able to have another opportunity to stay in America to achieve as much as I try. Looking back, those 6 months between January and June I studied really hard, and achieved very much in a short period of time. Starting with getting two 800s on both Math IIC and Chemistry, I got 2360 in my SAT reasoning test, and finally, I received the maximum score of 5 on all three AP tests I took in May. I felt that I could achieve anything if I tried hard enough.

My seventeen years of life so far brought many changes. And I have adjusted to those changes with much success. With that adjustability, I have a firm faith that I have a great potential to still grow and achieve yet more. Like the Nike commercial, impossible is nothing. Although many people might have thought that it was too late to suddenly change my path from going to a Korean college to going to an American college, I have set the first foot of this college process already, and I did it the right way. I am very proud of the amount of work I have done in a relatively short period of time and how much I have pulled out from those endless practices and strenuous work. Although I have only begun the first steps for the college entrance process in America, I do believe that I will do well in the future, and with support and love I have amassed from all my beloved people around me, without a doubt, I will grow stronger.

"My Life's Journey toward Greatness"

Kevin Kang

I am a first-generation Korean-American. My family was born in Korea, and so to explain my life, I have to explain where my parents are from. My parents came to America in 1987. Actually, my father came to America in 1984 to get started on his education in America. My father was born in 1961, so he was 23 when he came to America. His hometown, Busan, is located in the countryside of

Korea. My mother, however, was born in Jeju-do. Jeju-do is Korea's largest island and is located on the bottom of the Korean peninsula. When my father arrived in America, he attended Fairleigh Dickinson University. My mother was in Korea during the 2 years my father was at FDU, so those 2 years were extremely difficult for my parents since they were 13 hours plane-ride apart. My father eventually went back to Korea to marry my mother. They both decided that living in America was more beneficial for the family, so my parents permanently moved to America.

I can't even begin to fathom how difficult it must've been for my parents to leave their family and friends behind to start a new life in a new country, especially with the language barrier they must learn to overcome. After they moved to America, their first house was in Rutherford, New Jersey. I wasn't born yet, so I never lived in the house. During this time, my father was still continuing his studying and going for a major in computer science. My mother worked at Fort Lee Plaza Center. She was an assistant manager to a video store called *Sarangbang*. It was a Korean video store that recorded popular Korean television shows on VHS and allowed people to rent the shows for a fee. My father eventually joined my mom at *Sarangbang*, later becoming the manager of the video store. When my mother became pregnant, my parents decided they needed a bigger house so they could accommodate their newest family member, me.

Fort Lee, New Jersey had a bigger population of Koreans, making is easier for my parents to go about their daily lives. It was also closer to the *Sarangbang*, and since my father finished his education, he no longer needed to commute to the university.

On April 5th, 1992, my mom went to Englewood Hospital in Englewood, New Jersey and I was born at 12:01, April 6th, 1992.

I was first born as Kang Chang Mo (강창모). However, since I was born in America, my parents saw it befitting to give me an American name as well. Kevin Kang was my legal American name.

I was the first child my parents had, so of course my parents were overly enthusiastic to have a child. We stayed in Fort Lee for a few months because Fort Lee Plaza was a mere 5 minutes away. My parents took turns working at *Sarangbang*, one tending the video store, and the other taking care of me. My dad bought his new camera after I was born, so there are a slew of baby pictures of me. There's even a whole album dedicated to my saliva-dripping, finger sucking self. However, we moved out of the Fort Lee house shortly and moved to Palisades Park, another town heavily populated with Koreans, and only a few minutes away from Fort Lee and the Plaza. Even though the house was further away, the new house was much better than the the house in Fort Lee.

The only event I remember from this house was my one-year birthday party. In Korea, there is a tradition every child participates in when they turn 1. After the traditional party with family members, the attention is put on the birthday boy/girl. Laid out in front of him are four different objects. The belief is that whatever item the child chooses, it will be an indication of what he will expect in the future. The items are: pen for intellect, money for success, string for long life, and rice for good health. There are various other items people put in for variety, but these are the most commonly used.

As the attention shifted from the food and party to me, I was plopped on the middle of my hardwood floor. Laid out in front of me on a white cloth was a pen, a one dollar bill, grains of rice, and a piece of string. At first, I didn't understand what to do. I remember my father telling me that I crawled over to the other side, completely disregarding the items in front of me. After I was put back in place, I had to choose the item that would "determine my fate". To my parents delight, the item I grabbed was the pen. However, I ended up putting the pen in my mouth because it looked like an edible object. Not really the best way to start my quest for a great intellectual achievement, but to some extent that day's omen proved to be true as my life unfolded.

For the next three years, I stayed home, went to Korea for the first time, and went to Disneyworld in Florida. These memories are all very vague, having pictures to remind me, but one event I do remember is the birth of my brother. My brother was born on April 16th, 1996, four years and 10 days after I was born. I remember staying in a very big white room, while my mother was in her room. I had my beat up 3CPO action figure with me. After some time had passed, my father brought me into the hospital room so I could see my brother. My mom was lying straight up on her bed, and I remember seeing this tiny person, wondering where it came from. I tried to give it my 3CPO, but my mom stopped me, saying that I would have time to play with him later. My parents had already decided on his name. Kang Kyung Mo (강경모) and Andrew Kang.

A few months after my brother was born, we moved again, this time to Ridgefield, New Jersey, the place where I would spend the majority of my childhood. The first time I saw the house, I was amazed at how big it was. To my disappointment, the house was split into two. I learned this type of house was called a duplex, and I remember thinking how stupid the word "duplex" was. We lived on the upper floor, while the other family lived on the bottom floor. I was 5 years old at the time, so when we were moving, I tried to help out by moving as much luggage a 5 year old possibly could, but walking up those stairs while carrying my two-pound backpack was a struggle in itself. Even though the house was split into two, our house was significantly bigger than our previous one.

The house was like a mansion to a five year old. Right when you come in, there are four panels of giant windows right by the wall that gave a huge and amazing view of the outside. I would sometimes sit in front of the window, hypnotized by the view. It made the house seem more open and spacious. There was a kitchen, a playroom, a bathroom, and three bedrooms. I owned a bunk bed, which I shared with my brother. My brother and I had a fight over who would get the bottom bunk, and of course my brother won my mother's sympathy with his babyish charm. After some time, the downstairs family moved out, and a new family moved in. They were a family of 4, Korean, and had two kids similar to Andy's and my age. Little did I know, they would become my first friends.

When they first moved in, we awkwardly introduced ourselves to each other. The boy was named Brian and was one year younger than me. The girl was named Gina, and she was the same age as my brother. Since we lived literally two seconds apart, the majority of the time I spent in that house was with Brian, Gina, and my brother. We would do stupid kid activities like dress up or play hide and go seek. I remember for Halloween, we all dressed up as Teenage Mutant Ninja Turtles. Brian and me had an argument for an hour, regarding who would be Leonardo, the courageous leader of the group. To solve our dilemma, we did what any child would do in a difficult situation. Rock-Paper-Scissor. We lined up, putting everything on the line. After the fateful word "scissors", we placed our bet. I got paper. Brian got scissor. I was devastated. I had to dress up as the not as cool Michelangelo.

We were also young, avid gamers, playing video games but I became a video game addict when I received my Nintendo 64 as a Christmas present. It was Christmas morning, and I had just woken up to a white Christmas. Slowly opening my eyes, I turn my head to the right and see a huge red box. For a second, I was confused, wondering why there was a big red box next to my bed stand. Then it hit me. It was Christmas! I jumped out of bed, eagerly grabbed the red box and ran to the kitchen. Trying to locate a scissor, I opted for a fork, having no other sharp utensils around. I peeled the wrapping paper in about 2 seconds, and laid my eyes on a beautiful sight. It was a brand new Nintendo 64. It even had Mario 64 packaged in with it! I was ecstatic, immediately running downstairs to let Brian know. I enthusiastically knocked on his door. His mom opened the door, and I peered my head to the side and saw Brain playing his Nintendo 64! For a whole week, we both played our new gaming system nonstop. It got to the point where our parents got fed up about our constant playing. They took our Nintendo 64's away. Taking away my new Nintendo 64 was the worst punishment they could have given me. No matter how much I argued, they defiantly stood their ground and did not give me back my N64. Back then, I thought how unfair it was, but now I appreciate it. Limiting my time with the N64 helped me learn how to control my priorities.

Like the majority of Asian children, I started attending *hagwon* (an after school academy to boost study skills) The *hagwon* I attended was located in Palisades Park. I started in 1st grade because my mom wanted me to learn my study habits early on. The academy I attended was called M.E.K. (I still am not sure what the acronym stands for). The *hagwon* had its grand opening a few months before I started attending. It was located on Broad Ave, on the second floor of a dentist office. The *hagwon* was small, only consisting of 4 rooms, and a staff of about 6 teachers. Currently, M.E.K has expanded to three new buildings, and is one of the most successful *hagwons* in Palisades Park.

I dreaded coming to M.E.K. because I saw no point to it. I was a child, and I thought going to school was torture enough. Now I had to go to an after school program right AFTER school! Did my mom hate me? I was doing fine in school, and I didn't need any help with any of my schoolwork. Yet my mother insisted I take classes there. The first class I took was appropriately named Reading So

Great. This program focused on reading skills. The student would borrow a book from the Reading So Great "library", and after the student was finished with the book, he had to pass a 15-question test based on the book. A score lower than 10 was considered failing, and the book must be read again. Although I was skeptical, the program helped me to gain a love for reading and exposed me to a higher reading comprehension at an early age.

Every since then, I have been attending M.E.K. for at least one semester in the year and by attending M.E.K, it has helped me become a better student and also allowed me to meet my best friend, Jaewoo. He was the son of the director of M.E.K., and if I never attended M.E.K., I would've never made such a strong bond with Jaewoo. We had the same classes together, and my mom and his mom were quickly becoming friends. He was a shy kid, who wore oval shaped glasses and sported a bowl cut. Even though he lived in Palisades Park, we still managed to meet up and hang out. In the summer, while I was attending M.E.K., I would occasionally sleep over at his house. They became like a second family to me. I would go on summer camp trips with them, and he would come on summer trips with us. We attended the same summer camp and basically went everywhere with each other. Funny how people meet one of the most important people of their life in such unusual places.

M.E.K. also changed my life by exposing me to Mr. DePietro. Mr. DePietro was one of the first teachers at M.E.K. and I was blessed to be one of his first students at M.E.K. He was an English teacher but he was not like my teachers in elementary school. His way of teaching and interacting with his students was very unique. He actually made me enjoy learning, something no other teacher had ever done before. He was Italian, with a small afro, a scrunched up face, and a fat belly, but he was one of the funniest and most knowledgeable teachers I have ever had. He joked around and had a very sarcastic way of talking, which made him even funnier. He would poke fun at you, but everyone knew it was all good-hearted. Every class he would make us laugh, even cry from the laughter, while teaching us grammar and writing skills.

After I attended his class for a while, I started becoming more open and friendly with him, and we would jab jokes at one another. A relationship like that with a teacher was extremely beneficial. I looked at Mr. DePietro not as a teacher, but as a friend; a friend who was older, wiser, and funnier than I was.   He showed me the invaluable lesson that learning could be fun, and that classes could be entertaining. He made me appreciate writing, and show me how important grammar was. In a matter of weeks, Mr. DePietro converted me into a grammar enthusiast. To me, that is an extraordinary accomplishment, and I am extremely grateful to have a teacher like that in my academic life.

During the summer of 1999, I was allowed to go to Korea with two of my friends, Jinho and Jinuh. My parents could not go with me to Korea because they were too busy with their jobs, and Jinho's parents were too busy with their jobs as well. This was my second time in Korea, but it felt more like my first. As we got to the airport, I got out of the car with my little backpack bursting with toys and games. Squeezing my mother's hand, I was pretty nervous and excited because this was the first time I would be away from my parents for an extended period of time. I planned on staying in Korea for a month, two weeks with my *Chin Hal Ah Buh Gee* and *Chin Hal Muh Nee*, and two weeks with my *Wae Hal Muh Nee.*

My *Chin Hal Ah Buh Gee* and *Chin Hal Muh Nee* are my grandparents on my father's side and *Wae Hal Muh Nee* is my grandmother on my mother's side. My *Wae Hal Ah Buh Gee* passed away when I was 3, so I never had the chance to get to know him, so I wanted to take this chance to get to know all my grandparents before it was too late. Since I was a minor, the stewardess helped me find my seat and put my luggage away. I was initially horrified at the thought of flying. Nevertheless, I manned up and went on board. I even managed to stay calm the whole ride. I wanted to sleep because the plane ride was 13 hours, but I stayed awake, playing my Gameboy as entertainment. Jinho was passed out next to me, and Jinuh was quietly reading her book. I remember there was a movie playing, but it didn't look interesting enough to distract me from my Gameboy.

However, the next movie captured my attention. I didn't really pay too much mind to the movie in the beginning because I wasn't interested, but when I glanced up from my Pokemon battle, I saw a guy in a black coat and black sunglasses dodging bullets in slow motion. This one fateful scene had me mesmerized throughout the whole movie. Since I missed the beginning, I wasn't really aware what the plot was, and I didn't have any headphones either, which didn't help. Either way, I continued to watch the movie completely oblivious to the story or title. At the end of the movie, I asked the stewardess what the name of the movie was. It was called *The Matrix* and became my favorite movie of all time. Making a mental note of the movie, I closed my eyes and drifted away to sleep.

As we left the airport, I tried to locate my relatives. I was going to my father's family first. I walked out of the gate, I saw my grandmother and grandfather and about 10 other more relatives. I was surprised to see so many people, and they were all here for me! The only relatives I remembered were my grandparents and one aunt. Besides that, I had no recollection of any of my other relatives. The last time they had seen me was when I was two, but I was seven now. The first reaction I got was" You've grown so big!" They all hugged me exuberantly, especially one aunt, who was bigger than the rest, squeezing me until I couldn't breathe. Before leaving, I said good-bye to Jinho and Jinuh, who were going off with their grandparents. After a 30-minute wait for my luggage, we headed for the car. I arrived early in the morning and when I stepped out, I was greeted by a blazing sun and humid weather. It felt like someone put a wet cloth over my face. It was so hard breathe. Once we got into the car, after begging to turn on the air conditioner, I fell asleep as soon as I sat on the leather seats.

When I awoke, we were still on our way to my grandparent's house, which was located in Busan. Busan was a beautiful city. It was located on the southern-tip of the Korean peninsula, and is one of the busiest seaports in Korea. It currently is the 2nd biggest metropolis, next to Seoul. Back when I went, it wasn't the huge, bustling city it is now. There were a lot of people on the streets, some biking, some walking, and some running. There were even stray dogs and chickens running around the streets. The streets were unevenly paved, and some were completely inaccessible to cars. Since Busan was one of the biggest seaports in Korea, seafood was prominent. Every time I stepped outside, the smell of seafood was prevalent in the air. If not the smell of seafood, the stench of sewage overtook my senses. However, Busan still had traces of the country life-style.

As I looked out the windows, I saw pastures of green and mountains, something I had never seen in New Jersey. The one thing I don't remember seeing too much of were trees. My grandparent's house was located at the end of a long, grassy road. The road wasn't paved, so the ride was a bumpy one. When we arrived, the first thing I noticed was the open space in front of the house. There was a gate in the front, but it was never closed. When I walked into the house, it was very dimly lit, which made a very serene setting.

The first thing I saw was many tables and chairs and wondered why my grandparents would need so many. I soon found out that the house was not only a house, but also a restaurant. The bottom floor is for the customers, the second floor is a conference room for larger groups, and the third floor is where my grandparents, aunt, uncle, and two little cousins slept. The food is made in a basement, which acts like a big kitchen. At first glance, it looked like a dungeon, with its grey concrete floor and all the different types of machinery. There was only one door in and out, and there was always smoke coming out of it. There was a rectangular window, right above the stove so the food could get delivered. I helped out a few times but stopped after I carelessly burned my right hand on a stove.

My grandmother was the main cook. She had helpers, who were local women around the area, and had been working with my grandmother for years. To this date, I had never eaten Korean food better than my grandmother's.

The restaurant served traditional Korean food like *BiBimBap, Kimchee Chigae, DangJangJeeGae,* and other delicious dishes. My favorite, and also the customers' favorite, was her delicious *BiBimBap.* This dish consisted of rice, assorted vegetables, meat, eggs, sesame oil, and chili pepper paste. It was a "mixed" dish, where people needed to mix all the ingredients together to make this dish. The white rice would be on the bottom of the dish, with the vegetables on top. The hot eggs were put on top of the vegetables and a spoonful of chili pepper paste was put on top. A little bit of sesame oil was added to put more flavor in it. The vegetables included were cucumber, zucchini, mushroom, spinach, tofu, lettuce, bellflower root, and soybean sprouts. I always put 2 spoonfuls of chili pepper paste to make it extra spicy, and would always turn the *BiBimBap* to an extra shade of red. On lucky days, my grandmother would make *Dolsot BiBamBap*, which was *BiBimBap*, but in a very hot stone bowl. It was so hot that it could cook an uncooked egg. It kept the *BiBimBap* hot and fresh, and the sesame oil made the rice touching the bottom of the bowl brown and crispy. I would always save it for last, devouring it like a dessert.

When the restaurant was busy, I sometimes helped deliver dishes to customers. I would carry water, spices, or anything else customers asked for. I would grab the plastic cup from the dishwasher, fill it up with ice, walk over to the water cooler and hurry over to the customer. I would get on my tiptoes and place the water next to the customers' dish, waiting for a thank you. If the customer didn't say thank you, I stayed in the same spot until the customer did say thank you, or my grandmother took me away.

Throughout the day, there was always some sort of activity occurring in my grandparents' house, but after 8, when the restaurant closed, the activity slowed down to a crawl. There was no room for me to sleep on the third floor so I had to sleep downstairs, near the kitchen. I didn't mind sleeping downstairs because there was a cool breeze and it was less stuffy, but there was one thing that I despised about sleeping downstairs. Mosquitoes. Korea is infamous for their mosquitoes in the summer, and I learned first hand how annoying and bothersome they could be. The first night I slept downstairs, mosquitoes bit me everywhere, and it became a real nuisance. Sometimes I would wake up and see three or four mosquitoes buzzing around me, laughing at my useless attempts to swat them away with my mosquito-bitten arm. After two days, the mosquitoes became such a problem that my grandmother bought a mosquito net. The mosquito net was like a heaven-sent gift. It kept the nagging mosquitoes away from me, and allowed me to sleep peacefully throughout the night.

Besides the mosquito bites, there was really nothing else that bothered me about Korea. My time in Korea was easily one of the most memorable events in my life, not just because of the family I met, but because of all the history I learned. I visited historical monuments and gained knowledge about my past history through my relatives, especially my grandparents. Everything in Korea was radically different from America, the houses, streets, stores, restaurants, and just the lifestyle in general. Shopping was a totally new experience for me in Korea. Like America, Korea had supermarkets, but most people shopped at outdoor shopping centers. They were extremely hard to miss because hundreds of people would walk through the shopping area every day. There would be vendors spread all around the marketplace, selling seafood, vegetables, fruits, meats, and various other assortments of food. The stands were all tightly packed right next to each other, which would create medley of aromas. There was a roof over the whole marketplace, just in case it rained; however, it was still useful when it was unbearably sunny. The noise and commotion of the marketplace made the whole atmosphere very lively. The aroma of all the exotic foods mixed together was something I had never smelled before. The smell is very hard to describe because different sections had different smells. Of course the seafood section, which was the most prevalent throughout the shopping area, overpowered most of the other smells. There were some unpleasant aromas, like some of the raw meat. There was one section that smelled like sweaty socks. Despite these unusual scents, I accompanied my grandmother to the shop every time because I loved the atmosphere of the marketplace.

After two long eventful weeks in Busan, I had to go to Jeju-Do to meet my relatives on my mother's side. After I said my good-bye's and gave my hugs, I left with my uncle to the train station. What I didn't expect was a ferry ride to Jeju-Do. The ferry was my first time on any kind of boat and the view of the ocean was amazing. As I walked into the ferry, I saw rows and rows of benches. Going up the stairs, the door opened to a section that was outside. As I walked up the stairs, trying to maintain my balance on the rocking boat, I arrived on the top floor. Opening the door, a gush of wind pushed in, almost knocking me to the floor. Luckily my uncle was behind me, ready to catch my fall.

When I arrived in Jeju-Do, many of my relatives were present. As I got closer and closer to the shore, I could see about 7 people waiting for me. When the ferry docked, I could see all my uncles, aunts, and cousins waving enthusiastically. They too had not seen me since I was 2, and some had never seen me at all. After we all exchanged big hugs and handshakes, I followed my eldest aunt to her house, which was in a walking distance. My aunt was a pharmacist and owned her own pharmacy, which was located right underneath her apartment.

My cousins, Bong-Joo, Hyun-Ji, and Yoon-Ji were all older than me. It was summer break, and like America, my cousins were enjoying the summer. Out of all the amazing places in Jeju-Do, the most memorable event was the fishing trip we embarked on. Since Jeju-Do is an island, seafood is a big factor in Jeju-Do economy as well as lifestyle. Everywhere you turned, there was either a seafood related stand, or a shore. This was my first time fishing, and it definitely showed. I could barely hold onto the fishing rod, let alone reel a fish in. I did, however, with the help of my cousins, catch a small fish. After an interesting fishing trip, we went clam hunting on the beach.

Now at this I was more successful (I attribute the success to all the years of hide and go seek). I managed to find about 10 clams in a span of 20 minutes. I thought we were only catching clams for fun, but to my surprise we went back home and set up dinner. I was never a big fan of seafood, but since I had such a fun time catching the seafood, it would have been a shame not to get a treat after a hard day's work.

My uncle cooked the fish and clams, my aunt prepared the side dishes, and I sat at the table, nervous and anxious. The fish were done first, and as my uncle placed the fish onto my dish, I immediately bit into it. What a bad idea. I had a mouthful of burnt fish skin and fish bones. I saw my cousins laughing as I tried to spit out all the fish gunk I ate. Hoping that the clams would be better, I took out the clam meat and stuffed it into my mouth. It was one of the saltiest and unappetizing piece of food I have ever eaten. With a scrunched up face, I spit out the clam meat and begged for some water. I have never eaten another piece of clam meat in my life since; however, I did learn how properly to eat a fish.

I would occasionally visit my *Wae Hal Muh Nee* at her house, and slept one day overnight at her house. I couldn't stay with her the whole time because she would sometimes go to other places, and couldn't take care of me all the time. I tried to be as friendly as possible because I wanted to really get to know my grandmother. My Korean wasn't the best in the world, but I got by. At home, I knew how to say hello, food, and bye. I knew certain phrases that were commonly used in the house, but in Korea, I had to converse in Korean. Everyday I was learning new words, and my grandmother would help me read a book in Korean. By the end of the month, I was practically speaking Korean with a real Korean accent. This however did not last long. I was scheduled to leave Korea the next morning, and I was surprisingly sad to go. I had grown accustomed to the Korean lifestyle. The experience and knowledge I gained from Korea is something that has still stuck with me till this day. Although this trip was my most recent trip to Korea, I am anxiously waiting for my next trip to Korea. It was 11 years ago.

I headed back to the airport, sadly saying good-bye to all my relatives. Once I arrived at the airport, I met up with Jinho and Jinuh. After briefly talking with them about how their trip was, we boarded the plane, and I was more than ready to sleep through the 13-hour plane ride back home.

Walking up from an uncomfortable plane ride back, I still thought I was in Korea. However, looking around I saw that we arrived at JFK airport. Back in America, my parents decided to move again, but this time in the same town. The new house was on Clarks Ave, a couple of blocks away from our current house on Oak Street. We packed all of our things and brought it down to the car. Since the house was so close, we could take multiple trips back and forth moving the stuff. The positive aspect of moving to this house was that it was much closer to where all my friends lived during my elementary school days. There was Kris, Alex, Sang, Sung and eventually Andy. They all lived about 5 minutes away from my new house, and each had their own distinctive personality in the group.

Kris was the comedian in our group. He was half Filipino and half German, and had a very innocent nature about him. I met Kris in 2nd grade, but didn't become close friends with him until 3rd grade. He was always tall for his age, and was the skinniest out of the group. His skin looked paler than most, and he always had short messy hair. His parents owned and worked in a bakery store in Palisades Park, so he always had food at his house. Every time I slept over at his house, his mom would bring us baked goods from the store. She also made us popular Filipino food, my favorite being Chicken Adobo. It consisted of mainly chicken slowly cooked in soy sauce, vinegar, crushed garlic, bay leaf, and black peppercorns. She would always serve it over rice, and every time I took a bite of Chicken Adobo, I was in heaven. Every time I was over Kris's house, I prayed that his mom would make us Chicken Adobo. On the unlucky days she didn't, she still served us amazing Filipino food.

Kris was never great at school, but he was very athletic. He could outrun everyone, and because of his height, he was a one of the top basketball players in the school. Even though he was very athletic, he was a kid at heart. He was notorious for his pranks. He would spend a whole day perfecting a prank, and was not satisfied until his scheme worked. Kris loved to watch WWE. He even had a period where he was obsessed, talking and thinking about everyday. It was hard not to get caught up in his excitement, and he managed to convert all of us into wrestling fans. Kris showed me the humor and fun in life, something that should never be forgotten, regardless of any situation.

Kris was the humorous one, but when he was with Sang, they created a riot. Sang was Korean, and I met him in 3rd grade too. Sang was a short kid, with a bowl cut. He was on the "heavy" side, but so was I. He was the complete opposite of Kris physically. He wasn't very athletic, and was always very tan. He was the shortest one in our group, but had the loudest mouth. He was the joker in the group, but it was all in good fun. He loved making fun of people, especially fat kids, which was very hypocritical of him.

He lived near the school up until 4th grade. As fate would have it, Sang moved to the hill Kris lived on. The hill became our hotspot, as we met countless nights together on top of the hill. Most weekends, we would go to Kris's house, but end up in Sang's house.

Sang's house was a child's dream room. He was the "nerd" in our group, being the most technologically savvy. He always owned a minimum of 4 computers, which could all be connected together. He was also the first one to get the latest video gaming system. If we wanted to play some Xbox – Sang's house. If we wanted to play some PS2 – Sang's house. We had numerous all-nighters at Sang's house, either playing Counter-Strike on PC or Halo on Xbox. At the time, Sang's home was the place to be.

After I met Sang and Kris in school, I met Sung but in Church. Initially, we were just church friends, occasionally saying hi to one another, but in 3rd grade he moved to Ridgefield. We were put in the same class, and I was two seats away from Sung. He always had a tan because he was always outside. He hated staying home, and wanted to do some sort of activity. He originally wasn't in our group, but later became a part of our group after he moved closer to where we all lived. He had a friendly personality, but he did get annoying sometimes. He always had the idea that he had to talk, and that sometimes would get on all of our nerves. His family and my family became friends after we became friends, so I was invited to his house many times and he was invited to my house many times too. We would occasionally be invited to barbeque parties, where either my parents hosted or their parents did. Since Sung was an outdoors kid, we would always go to the park to play. We both got along fine until 4th grade, until problems began to arise.

Alex came to Ridgefield during 4th grade, and we quickly became friends. He moved to Hamilton Street, just a block away from where I lived. He was a nice kid, but if you got on his bad side, he would let you know that he didn't like you. He would ignore you, not talk to you, or just gave you a smug look He had a very boisterous personality, and for a 4th grader was pretty strong. He was easily annoyed, and had a very stubborn nature. Since the beginning, Alex had a sort of problem with Sung. He flat out stated that he didn't like Sung, and he convinced all of us to hate Sung too.

Whenever we hung out, Alex never came if Sung was around. Sung must have known that Alex did not like him because whenever Sung saw us with Alex, he pretended he never saw us. I had always liked Alex a bit more than Sung, but not enough to completely alienate Sung. He had his flaws but so does everyone else. Now that I think back on it, I was very stupid for doing what I did. One day walking to school, we told Sung that we didn't want to be his friends anymore, and at that time I didn't think anything of it, but now I regret it immensely. I shouldn't have listened to Alex, and I should've thought more about Sung because after we split up, he didn't have that many friends to go to since our elementary school was very small. I should've went with what I thought was right. We made Sung become a loner, and we even started picking on him by calling him names, which I think back in disgust. The worst thing we did though was the complete disregard for Sung. We acted like he wasn't there, like a ghost. He eventually moved out of Ridgefield, I don't know if it was because of us or because of his family, but I never got to say bye to Sung. However, I did meet Sung a few years later, during high school, and amazingly became friends again. It wasn't the same as back in Elementary school, but I was still glad to have him back as a friend.

After all this needless drama ensued, I met a new friend, and who would become one of my best friends in the future. Andy came to Ridgefield in 5th grade, but we quickly became good friends. He was born in Korea, but raised in California, so living in New Jersey was a completely new experience for him. He became friends with my other friend, So Young, first because they were in the same class together. Since So Young was a mutual friend, we met occasionally, greeting each other awkwardly each time we met. However, after a few more meet up's, we sparked a friendship.

Back then, he was a short kid, with highlighted hair, which he spiked up. Andy was known for his hair, and his massive amount of gel he would use. He had a very amicable personality, getting along with everyone he met. He always lent a helping hand, and would always try his best in everything he did. He even became class president, even though he had been in New Jersey for only 2 months.

He really did inspire me to work hard because he always worked diligently on his work.

Even though Andy was this overall caring guy, Alex somehow had a problem with him. Although I sided with Alex on Sung, there was no way I could side with Alex on this one. Alex would get angry whenever I hung out with Andy. I guess it made him feel a little jealous, but I couldn't ditch Andy to hang out with Alex. I started hanging out with Andy more often than Alex. I eventually told him that I would rather hang out with Andy then with him, so we went our separate ways. I still talk to Alex whenever I meet him because we both know that what happened was such a long time ago, but I still maintain close contract with Andy.

When there were no ill feelings for one another, we actually had a very enjoyable time. The trip to Lowes Theater in Ridgefield Park was a weekly event for us. If a new movie came out, we would have one of our parents drive us to Lowes Theater, drop us off, and someone else's parents would come pick us up after we were done. We sometimes arrived earlier so we could play at the arcade. There were the usual games, but to us, there was one machine we always played. The Pump It Up dance machine. It was similar to DDR, but instead of having four arrows on the floor, there were five. It became sort of an obsession for us. We even went as far as buying a smaller, home-friendly version of the game, just so we could play it. After playing in the arcade for a while, we would go see the movie, sometimes sneaking into the theater. And if the movie was R-rated, we found a way to get ourselves into the movie.

There was one day where we movie hopped, going from one movie to the next, and saw four movies in a row. After that, I stopped going to the movies for a while because of the amount of films I saw that day.

When we weren't at the movie theater, we were at the park. Ridgefield's park was walking distance from my house, so we would all meet up and head towards the park. There was a basketball court, tennis court, and baseball court. There was also a new playground installed when I was in 5th grade, so the park had everything a child needed. Our usual day consisted of basketball games and football games. I was never really good at basketball and I was decent at football, but I was really good at tennis. Tennis was my main sport in Elementary school, but overtime I lost interest in it. I do wish though that I did continue with the sport.

The park was a place to play sports, but it also catered to on other thing. The Youth Center, located in the middle of the park, was a place for kids to hang out. Its main purpose was to deter kids away from drugs and other substance abuses by having a place where kids can hang out, but to me, it was a place where I could get Pepsi at 50 cents and some Mrs. Fields Chocolate Chip Cookies for another 25 cents. The first thing you notice when you step foot in the Youth Center is the Foosball table. Next to the table are a couple of sofas. In front of each sofa is a television set, and each is connected to a game console. At the far end of the room, there are three pool tables set up. In the corner, there is a huge television connected to cable. It was like a mini-bar for children. It was only open Fridays and Saturday from 6 to 11 and we were there almost every weekend. It was a relaxing place to hang out, have a couple of sodas, and play some video games and some billiards. It definitely kept us busy during the weekends. After we were done hanging out at the Youth Center or playing in the park, we all headed back home, together.

Similarly, like the Youth Center helped me make smart choices in my life, my change in religion helped me shape my decisions in the future. I was born a Catholic, and raised as a Catholic. I was baptized at an early age. However, I was never really that religious, and only attended Church on special occasions. I never participated in any of the religious holidays like Lent, and attended Mass sporadically. The Church I attended was located in Saddlebrook, New Jersey, and the main reason I did attend Church was because some of my friends attended the Church. I never gained a personal connection with God, maybe because I never took the time to fully understand and read the bible, or maybe because I always never believed in it. Either way, I knew that I would never become a good Catholic or believe in its teachings.

One day, I was over at Andy's house, as were my two cousins, Jonathan and Dustin. They were headed out to a Buddhist Temple, located in Tappan. Back then, I had no idea what Buddhism was. The only image that came to my mind when thinking of Buddhism was a fat guy with a baldhead smiling, and if you rubbed his belly it brought good fortune. I was actually pretty curious as to what Buddhism actually was, and since I wasn't a devoted Catholic, I thought to myself I had nothing to lose.

It was Buddha's birthday, and the nightly ceremonies were being held at around 8. I asked my mother if I could spend the night at Andy's house as well as going to the nightly ceremony. To my surprise, my mother was very supportive of me going. I later found out that my parents were Buddhist back in Korea, but had to convert to Catholicism because there were no known temples around.

The temple is located right next to Tappan Golf Course, and is off a very busy street. When you enter, there is a dirt road leading to an old fashioned house. It looked nothing like the temples in Korea, but it was New Jersey, so I overlooked it. When we parked alongside the grass, I saw dozens of cars parked everywhere. I even saw a friend of mine from school there. I suddenly realized that there were other religions besides Christianity and Catholicism. I followed my cousin and Andy upstairs to the Youth Group section. To my amazement, I saw around 20-30 kids huddled around in the room. The youth group had less than my previous church's Youth Group, but I was astonished to see so many young Buddhists.

After I introduced myself to everyone in the group, our *Seaneem* (Monk) came in to greet us. His name was *Jin Hoo Seaneem*. I always thought monks were quiet and serious, but *Jin Hoo Seaneem* was the complete opposite. He was very loud and had a playful side to him. He was also in a top physical condition and had a very defined jaw line. Like all monks he had his head shaved and wore a brown robe. Since coming back from Korea, I had forgotten most of the Korean I had learned, and had trouble understanding *Jin Hoo Seaneem* because he was from Korea and only spoke Korean. Whereas I spoke broken Korean, he spoke broken English, so our first encounter was a very awkward one.

However, I still managed to initiate a conversation with *Jin Hoo Seaneem*, and I introduced myself to him. After meeting with everyone, we headed downstairs to the kitchen. In the kitchen, a *seaneem* gave me a glowing candle to hold. As we walked outside, I saw people line up behind the head *seaneem* and I quickly got on line behind everyone. It was around 9:30 when we started walking around the temple, slowly. While we were walking, the *seaneem*'s started chanting, and everyone else started chanting as well. Since I was new to Buddhism, I was completely oblivious to what they were saying, and I started mumbling to the words. We walked around the temple a few times, carrying the candles and chanting, and I thought to myself how unusual it was, but also how soothing it was as well.

Just walking around the temple, listening to the chants, I felt a sort of relaxation and calmness. Buddhism mystified me because even though I had no prior knowledge or experience with it, I still felt the aura and the power of it. After that day, I started going to *Jul* (Buddhist Temple) regularly, and after a while, started understanding what Buddhism was. I understood that Buddhism wasn't just a religion; it was a way of life. Buddhism is something that can be incorporated into daily life. The lessons I learned from Buddhism has not only changed my life, it has completely changed my way of thinking and viewing the world. Small ideas like not killing anything living, or eating everything on one's plate, has made me more aware of myself and aware of the world. I might not know everything there is to know about Buddhism, or completely understand it, but I try everyday to learn from it and also understand other religions. I'm not hateful towards Christians or Catholics, and I don't get mad when they try to tell me to convert to Christianity. Buddhism has taught me always to take a step back and look at the situation and act accordingly. It has made me a more level headed and calm individual and I am grateful for that.

After my change in religion, my family soon followed. My mother was the first to come with me to *Jul*, then my brother and then my father. Now my mother is on the committee of mothers at the *Jul*, and is also on the choir group. My brother is one of the younger ones in the Youth Group, but still attends *Jul*. My father was never very religious, so he comes during the major events or when we drag him along. I try to attend every week, but to me, it's not attending *Jul* that is the most important, but practicing what Buddha preaches and faithfully doing them.

My change in religion occurred in 6th grade, but another drastic change was about to happen. In the summer of 6th grade, I was hit with some news. I was moving. I wasn't new to moving, and at first, when my mother mentioned it, I shrugged it off, thinking I was moving to a new house somewhere in Bergen County. However, I was moving to Rockland County. A county I never heard of, and back then never wanted to go to. I left Ridgefield and moved to New City, New York. It was a very suburban town, with a large population of Jewish and middle class whites. In Ridgefield, most of my friends were Korean, so I wasn't sure how I would do in a mostly white town. At first, I was reluctant to go. I was leaving all my friends and teachers to go to this new, unfamiliar town. Even the town name New City seemed rather silly to me. On August 4th, 2003, I moved from my house in Ridgefield, to a new, unfamiliar, and unwanted house in New City.

It was a 40 minutes drive to New City. During the whole ride, I was in a gloomy mood. Thinking that if I stayed in a sour mood, my parents would feel bad and turn around. I was hoping they would say to me, "We're sorry Kevin. We're sorry for making you leave your friends, and making you move to this new town." I was hoping the new house would get destroyed, or something go wrong so that I could go back to Ridgefield. But it was all a sad child's dream.

Turning onto Scarlett Court, I see some apartment buildings to the bottom left of the road, and some houses to the right. I see a dead end sign, and thought how perfectly that sign explained my feelings.

To be honest, the house was better than I had expected it to be. It was definitely the best house I lived in, but it was in the middle of nowhere. Our area was a cul-de-sac, and I felt very closed in. Not knowing anyone around the area, I felt lonely.

Getting out of the car, I saw a big balcony coming out of the side of the house, a decent sized backyard and front yard. The house had two stories, a basement, and a top floor, with 4 bedrooms, 2 bathrooms, and a kitchen. And it looked like every other house on the block.

For the remaining summer, I stayed home and did nothing. I visited Ridgefield often, but the ride was too long for my parents to drop me off there everyday. After everything was set up, visiting IKEA countless times, until it finally looked right for my father. To celebrate we had a house party and invited my aunts, uncle, and cousins.

I told my cousins straight out, there was nothing to do. We couldn't set up the television or the computer because something was wrong with the basement's electrical sockets. I don't know why my mother never told me this before, but there was a mall very close to my house. The Palisades Center Mall is about 10 minutes from my house, and is the second biggest mall in America. Why I never knew about this mall before, I never know, but we begged our parents to take us. After some talk, we got my mother to drive us to the mall.

It went up four staggering stories, with rows and rows of shops. On the top floor was the "entertainment" floor, with dozens of restaurants and a movie theater. After browsing the 2nd biggest mall in America, we decided to watch *Anchorman: The Story of Ron Burgundy*. Arriving back home, I realized Rockland County wasn't as bad as I made it out to be, but in a few weeks, school would start. It was a blessing and a curse.

September 5th was the judgment day, my first day of school in New City. For the first time in my young life, I had to ride a bus to school. In Ridgefield, I walked to school or had my parents drop me off. In New City, I had to ride a bus because the school, Felix Festa Middle School, was too far for me to walk to and my parents wouldn't drive me because they felt it would help me interact with the students better. I woke up at 7:30, and took the long, faithful walk to my bus stop, which was surprisingly far. My bus stop was in front of another students house, and he happened to be in the same grade as I was. For a 7th grader, he was strongly built. After an awkward greeting, we introduced each other. His name was John and he was Russian. John became my first friend in New City.

8:00, the bus arrived. The minute I got on, I see only three kids sitting on the bus. Relived that I was one of the first stops on the bus route, and didn't have to try and find a seat, like the new kids do in movies. I sat up front, knowing that the older grades sit in the back. Arriving at the school, I saw hundreds of kids, some looking distraught, others looking anxious, but all chatty; I got off my bus and quietly went inside the school. Looking around and waiting for the bell, I saw old friends reuniting, and old schoolmates greeting each other. By the end of the school day, I met one new friend, but I met my new best friend on my way home.

After my first day in school, I anxiously waited to get off the bus and go home. However, as I was getting ready to get off the bus, I saw another kid in front of me get off at the same stop. Walking home, I quietly walked behind him. He would occasionally turn around and give me a questioning look, wondering who the heck I was. For 10 minutes, we quietly walked home. At the fork on Scarlett Court, he finally went left, while I went right. This moment happened for about a week, both of us awkwardly walking home together. However, one day I mustered the courage to spark a conversation with him.

I got off the bus earlier then he did, and started walking. I strategically started walking slower, and slower until I was walking right by him. As I was about to say something, he asked, "Are you new?"

This caught me by surprise, since I wasn't expecting him to talk after a week of silence. I quickly answered, "Yes".

We talked the whole way back. I found out his name was Kenan, and he would become my best friend in New York. He lived in New City most of his life. He was born in Bosnia, and came over to America in 2nd grade. He was about my size, but skinnier. He had dirty blonde hair, and wore uneven oval glasses. He lived in the apartment complexes on Scarlett Court, 30 seconds away from my house. He was a nice kid, with a caring personality. My first impression of him was completely off because I based it on our previous "interactions". To me, he seemed aloof and arrogant, but in reality he was the complete opposite of that.

Walking down the end of Scarlett Court, we both said our good byes and went home. The minute I arrived home, I informed my mom that I made a new friend. She wasn't used to me not having any non-Asian friends and was surprised that I made friends with Kenan.

Kenan also introduced me to all of his friends. Jon, Garrett, and Mike. I first met them at the lunch table in Felix Festa. I originally sat in the right hand corner of the room with 4 other kids. The 4 other kids were all new, and like me, knew no one. To my relief, I was finally allowed into a "lunch table". Before then, eating lunch was the most dreadful part of the day. Before school started, the constant worry of me not finding a "table" to sit at worried me greatly. Becoming friends with Kenan automatically made me friends with his friends.

Mike was the third friend I made, and he was Puerto Rican. I met him on the bus ride back to Kenan's house. He was extremely laid back and calm. He never had much interest in school, failing most of the classes, but he was not dumb. He just never had much motivation to do well. His parents divorced at a young age, and Mike had to commute back and forth between his mother and father. It was difficult for him, and the stress of schoolwork did not help.

Like Mike, Jon had a unique family. He was born in Illinois, but was later adopted by Mr. & Mrs. Goldsmith. I never asked why or how Jon was adopted because I felt it was an uncomfortable question to ask. He had dark brown hair, massive arms and legs, and wore glasses. Even though Jon was in 8th grade, he looked like he was already in high school. When you got to know Jon, he was really friendly and jubilant, but he did act arrogant on some occasions. He was an athlete, and would brag about his sports achievements. He would tell us how many homeruns he hit in his last game, or how many basses he stole last season. Arrogant people always annoyed me. However, I didn't have much of a choice to where I could sit, so I dealt with it.

Garrett was an odd one. He was tall, lean, and handsome. He had blond hair, swished over to the right side of his face. However, he had one of the most selfish personalities I have ever seen. Sometimes, he was a real nice guy, but on other days, he made it seem like the world revolved around him. He wasn't the brightest kid either, failing multiple classes one year. I'm the type of person that could never hate anyone, and although Garrett got on my nerves, he was the best friend of Kenan. I learned to deal with his ways, and actually became quite close with him.

There was one thing that Kenan, Mike, Garrett, and Jon had in common. They all knew how to snowboard.

Around 8th grade, I discovered my love for snowboarding, thanks to my friends. Before 8th grade, I was terrible at any snow activity, be it skiing, snowboarding, or even tubing. I first started off skiing, due to my parents. I was about 12, on top of a mountain, with my knees trembling. I hated the sharp pain from the cold stinging wind, and my snow pants were cold from the wet snow puddle I previously "stumbled" into. I was miserable.

Looking down the mountain, I knew I would not be able to survive this trip down. Clutching my ski poles, I formed a pizza shape with my skis (like my instructor told me to) and slowly, SLOWLY, wiggled my way down. Going from side to side, I was beginning to get the hang of it. Thinking I would be able to go straight down, I turned and was sadly awakened. One of my edges caught on the snow, and I tumbled down. Both ski poles blasted off my feet, and I lay in the snow, humiliated. As I was getting up, I noticed a sign. It read "Kid Mountain." This mountain wasn't even a mountain, it was a hill designed for kids 2-10. This huge and dreadful mountain was a small hill that 5 year olds went on to practice. Embarrassed, I quickly got up, collected my ski poles and headed back to the lodge. After that day, I promised myself I would never ski again.

However, a few years later, I was back on snow, but not on skis. I was at Mountain Creek Ski Resort in New Jersey, ready to snowboard. I had my new Burton Jacket, Oakley beanie, and Spyder snow pants. Remembering my past experiences with snow sports, I was unenthusiastic about going. The only pushing force for me going snowboarding was that it was easier than skiing. How wrong I was.

At the snowboard rental area, they asked me if I was goofy or regular. Not knowing anything about snowboarding or skateboarding, I replied regular, too embarrassed to ask what that meant. Stepping outside to the brisk December air, I was ready to risk my life again. Sinking into the knee-deep pile of snow, I made my way to the Cabriolet. Kicking off the snow, I stepped into the Cabriolet with my two cousins and Kenan. Jonathan and Dustin have been snowboarding for roughly a year, while Kenan has been for two years. They were going to teach me how to snowboard, and this was on an actual mountain.

Although I would like to say that I wasn't scared, I can't because I was terrified. My past memories of all the falls and bruises due to skiing came rushing back. Getting off the lift, I clumsily walked down to the strap in the area. I threw my snowboard into the soft snow and tried to strap in. Trying to make myself seem like less of a novice, I didn't ask for help, but honestly I had no idea what I was doing. Wearing my big Gore-Tex gloves, I tried and failed to strap my boots into the bindings. To make things worse, snow kept on piling up on the binding because the snowboard wouldn't stay still. I couldn't believe I was already having this much trouble. Finally strapping in, I got up and tried to stop.

However, I started to slide down. I was like an elephant on an ice rink. I couldn't control where I was going. Since I didn't know how to stop, I did the one thing I knew how to do. I fell, straight on my butt. Holding my butt in pain, Dustin rode over and helped me up. He told me I needed to learn how to stop before shooting down the mountain like I did. I tried to tell him that I didn't want that to happen either, but he rode away before I could say anything. As I tried to ride down the mountain, Kenan stopped me and showed me how to stop. He told me that unless I knew how to stop, I would never learn how to snowboard. He showed me the heel-side stop first, which is when you stop with your heels and have your body looking down at the mountain. Trying to imitate Kenan, I pushed my right foot forward to try and make myself face the mountain. Kenan told me that I needed to bend my legs and push my butt out. Following his advice, I leaned back and stuck my butt out. I ended up falling on the same spot I fell before. For a whole hour, I practiced stopping heel-side, and somehow managed to get to the bottom of the mountain, even if I did fall most of the way down.

Strapping out of my board, I told Dustin that the board didn't feel right. He told me that I was probably a goofy, not a regular. Goofy was when your right foot is in front, and regular is when your left foot is in front. With this new knowledge, I went back to the rental area and exchanged my board for a goofy one. After another 3 hours of continuous falling, I learned how to stop toe-side and heel-side. At the end of the day, I managed to learn how to snowboard and not kill myself! Even though I couldn't sit down for a few days, it was worth it.

Ever since then, I've been snowboarding every winter. I've bought a season pass to mountain creek for the last 4 seasons, and go up to Mountain Creek at least once a week. I even helped start a snowboarding club in my High school.

Snowboarding has become a big part of my life. It has made winter my favorite season and snow my favorite type of precipitation. When it snows, I don't think about school cancellations, I think about where I could snowboard. The snowboard lifestyle and culture has always captivated me. From subscribing to snowboarding magazine to buying snowboarding videos, I was immersed in snowboarding.

Similarly to how snowboarding changed my life, meeting my blind cousin has changed my perspective on life.

It was Wednesday night at 8:00 P.M, and my heart was pounding as I waited anxiously in front of the customs gate at JFK; I was unaware that I am about to meet one of the most influential people of my life. She was scheduled to arrive at 7:45, but it was already half-past eight, and she was still a no show. Tapping my feet to the beat of Kanye West's "Stronger," I figured she was being escorted out of the plane and receiving extra attention not because she was famous, but because she was blind. After all, aren't all blind people helpless? This myth I had conjured up in my mind, however, was soon to be shattered.

This was JuHyun's first time in the states, and she was here to audition for Performing Arts schools like Julliard and Berklee. She was going to stay at my house for a month. I had never met or seen her before, and I was nervous because I had never dealt with a blind person before, let alone lived with one. For 30 minutes, I contemplated what I would say to her. Suddenly out of the corner of my eye, I saw a well-dressed tall lady walk out with a small Asian girl clinging to her arm. JuHyun was here, and I was still nervous. Slowly making my way towards them, I greeted them with an awkward handshake. The well-dressed lady, Mary, was JuHyun's foster parent. Thinking that I *had* to help JuHyun, I quickly offered to take all of her luggage. To my surprise, she refused the offer politely, and we walked quietly to the car.

The first week of her stay was filled with uneasy interactions and conversation. Thinking of only myself, I made various excuses to be out of the house when JuHyun was there. My mom must have seen the stilted interaction between JuHyun and me because she ordered me to go shopping with her at Woodbury Commons the following Sunday. Little did I know, that this day would become the most eye-opening day of my life.

Arriving at Woodbury, I reluctantly got out of the car. JuHyun needed new shoes so our first stop was Payless. Scouring through many shoes, I immediately went to the most fashionable pairs. What 21-year old woman would not love some fashionable shoes? Due to my naïveté and selfish thinking, I didn't realize that the shoes JuHyun needed were supposed to be comfortable walking shoes. I picked out high-heeled, strappy shoes. I brought some over to JuHyun, and was confident that she would have loved the shoes, but she told me that she could not wear those types of shoes. I made an assumption that JuHyun would love the shoes, only based upon my opinion. Mary told me that JuHyun needed shoes that were closed-toe, in the case of rain. They also needed to be easy to wear and comfortable. The lacing system would have made putting on the shoes too time-consuming, and the lifted heel was unsuitable to be worn everywhere. I failed to put myself in her shoes and understand that she needed something comfortable that could be worn anywhere.

Shopping with JuHyun initially started out as a dreadful event, but at the end, my thoughts and views of others radically changed. Shopping with JuHyun made me aware of not only blind people, but also anyone different. I never imagined myself in another person's position, always thinking of myself. I admired the patience that Mary possessed when dealing with JuHyun and the understanding she had of her. The difficulties that JuHyun faced, even with something simple as shopping, made all my own difficulties that I faced infinitesimal. JuHyun helped me become more mature and taught me the compassion and understanding towards people who were different. JuHyun wasn't the blind one, I was.

Looking back now, I couldn't be happier on how my life turned out. I met wonderful people, and had some life changing events. I have become responsible and mature, and as I get older and get closer to college, I look forward to the wondrous and uncharted course my life will take.

"Into the Arms of Historical Significance"

David Yun

It was the twenty-third of October and the year was 1992. I leaned back and rested my heavy head against the cushion of the wall. I was at peace, blissfully ignorant of time, authority, and responsibility. Little did I know that my everlasting paradise was soon to be besieged. All of a sudden I was violently interrupted as I was ripped from my mother and exposed to the world. That misfortune took place in a doctor's office in Queens, New York. I screamed. I kicked and I wriggled, demanding that I be put back. You should have seen the fight I put up. I opened my eyes to discover large blurs affectionately cooing at me. The trauma wore me out; I fell asleep.

There I lay on top of a soft bundle of cloth, surrounded by glass walls on all sides. I kept my eyes shut, trying to escape back into the safe haven of my mother's womb. It was pointless to open my eyes because all my vision offered was a fuzzy black and white window into the world. In the hospital room were my father, mother, aunt, uncle, and grandmother.

I woke up to the gentle murmur of the television set and found myself in a small apartment in Flushing, New York. I observed my new surroundings and came across a stocky Korean man with humorously unkempt hair and a slim Korean woman in a gaudy dress staring intently at me. They exchanged kind words and looked back to smile at me with complete adoration.

The man's name was Dad and the woman's name was Mom. I was pleased with this discovery and rewarded the two with a smile and a pool of drool. In the corner of my eye I saw a small figure bumble across the floor and eventually make its way towards me. It struggled to climb up the mattress, but its voracious curiosity propelled the tiny figure upwards. I stared back nervously as a pair of big bright mismatching eyes peered back with amusement. I discovered that the figure was only an adventurous little Korean girl. She looked content, as if her knowledge of my existence was some sort of award for her growing sense of cognition. The couple slowly pronounced the name of the girl to me: J-O-A-N-N-E. So the day ended with the acquisition of the fact that I have a Mom, Dad, and a Joanne.

The sun rose and its rays filtered through the smudged windows to hit my face. The year was 1996 and it was my first morning as a kindergarten student. I remember feeling an amalgam of excitement and fear. I have always overheard of this place called "kindergarten", but never ventured past rumors. I could only paint how it would look like in my mind. My four-year old mind envisioned it as a place where strict rules would apply, and the separation from my mother would occur. My mother would dress me back in those days. I always hated the clothes she picked out for me; hideous plaid flannel shirts tucked under my corduroy pants. My hair fell victim every morning to my mother's ritual grooming. So, with the picture of an institute of discipline in my head, an apple in my hand, and my Power Rangers lunch box clenched tightly in my other fist, I made my first foray into the American education system.

When I arrived at the school house, I suddenly felt frightened. My mother walked me inside the school, talked for a while to a teacher and dissipated into the crowds of watchful parents. I assumed that my mother abandoned me, as if I was being punished for a sin I had committed. I looked desperately for my mother's familiar sun dress, but my mind tangled from such fervent searching. I did what any frightened four-year old would do; I cried. I sat on the tiled floor and let a stream of tears flow down my scrunched face. It was amazing because as soon as I inhaled for my second tearful scream, my mother's hands appeared out of nowhere and picked me up from the ground. I felt safe again. My mother comforted me until my tears stopped gushing out from my eyes and set me down. Then she smiled at me and said, "Don't be afraid; it's just kindergarten. I'll be home when you get back". She disappeared into the dense parade of parents again and I was alone once more.

I slowly made my way over to my table, already inhabited by other children. They looked equally as dissatisfied as I did, with their pouted lips, scrunched faces, and lack of communication. I found my seat next to a little girl with blond hair. I had never seen such hair before, so I was astonished. For my entire life up until that moment, I have only seen the uniform black mane of the Korean population. Then, as I was studying the bleached hair, the head suddenly whipped around and revealed a pair of icy blue eyes piercing into my stare. After a minute of uneasy staring, she finally blurted out, "Hi! I'm Hanna. What's your name?" I literally did not know what to say. I have not been exposed to the English language, before. I was lost for words. What could I have possible offered as a response to the seemingly alien language? So, again, I did what any confused four-year old would do. I cried.

Of course, eventually I got used to the whole idea of being apart from my mother and started to enjoy school. During the school year of 1997, I was in the first grade in Public School 79. I enjoyed the colorful walls of my classroom, the kind teachers, and the fun activities associated with being a first grader. One teacher who I remember very clearly was Mrs. Marcus. She was my teacher, and Mrs. Marcus was quite possibly the kindest soul ever to supervise me.

Mrs. Marcus was a short, middle aged woman with a brown beehive of hair sitting on top of her head. When ever she smiled, her face would scrunch up into a mass of wrinkles. I remember this because she seemed happy every hour of the day. Mrs. Marcus would let our class spend the entire day just doodling on scrap paper. She would hand out colorful construction paper to everyone and let us raid the crayon cabinet. Mrs. Marcus strolled down through the aisles to laud our primitive art. She would always compliment my sloppy scribbles I proudly called "art" with the most genuine voice. When class ended and my parents arrived to take me home, I would always overhear Mrs. Marcus telling my parents how brilliant I was. Of course she was just being nice, but I believed her words to the very last letter. I guess that self-confidence really helped me out because I started to talk to my classmates more often and express myself more. However, all of Mrs. Marcus's encouragement and nurturing dissipated from my life when I entered the second grade.

Her name was Mrs. Noodleman, and she was a beast of a woman. She was also my second grade teacher. 1997 drifted on to 1998, and I just got promoted to the ranks of the second grade. The general of this army called "second grade" was Mrs. Noodleman. She was the perfect antithesis to Mrs. Marcus. Through my round six-year-old eyes, I saw Mrs. Noodleman having both the height and the heft of a massive water tower. She always looked exhausted as if she just ran a marathon. Of course, a light walk down the classroom aisles would qualify as a marathon for her.

She would sit herself down in her large chair and only leave it to get a snack. She would spend so much time stuck to that chair that I started to believe that the chair was a part of her body. After a few days of observing Mrs. Noodleman and her affinity to stagnancy, I decided to find out what was so enticing about that large chair. The next morning I arrived early to satisfy my curiosity concerning Mrs. Noodleman's chair. I waited until she got up to get a snack and cautiously made my way to the big chair. The climb up to the chair seemed impossible, but eventually I made my way up the tall chair and into the wide seat. I could not help but grin at the fact that I finally sat in the mighty Mrs. Noodleman's seat.

My sense of accomplishment was soon destroyed when Mrs. Noodleman suddenly appeared before me. She stood there with her hands on her barrel-like hips and eyes set to burn through my crime. I desperately searched for an inch of mercy on her now bright red face. But when Mrs. Noodleman was agitated, all signs of compassion fled from her face. I remember this because Mrs. Noodleman was always agitated. Before I could even explain myself, Mrs. Noodleman assigned detention to me and demanded to speak with my parents. She even pasted a piece of paper with the words, "David Yun has detention for disobeying the teacher" onto the main doorway so everybody could see that I committed the crime.

After all the children joyfully skipped along to their homes, I woefully sank down into my seat and waited for Mrs. Noodleman to finish telling my parents about how terrible I was. I could hear her heated tongue, rambling on through peaks and valleys of pitch. Her voice was probably the only agile thing about that woman. Anyway, I sat on my seat, filled with remorse and guilt. Finally, my parents emerged from the conference room and they both looked furious. But the strange thing was, Mrs. Noodleman also came out screaming at my parents. Fortunately, my six-year old brain was developed enough to deduce that my parents disagreed with what Mrs. Noodleman said. And what Mrs. Noodleman had been screaming for the past hour was that I am a rotten boy. So in that case, my parents must have been defending me in that conference room. All of a sudden, my guilt melted away as I followed my parents to the car and went home.

After a year of Mrs. Noodleman and her vengeful oppression over me, I escaped to the third grade in 1999. I have to be honest; the trauma of the second grade left me a little pessimistic about school. I assumed that from now on, all elementary school teachers would be as abominable as Mrs. Noodleman. I ruminated about the atrocities of the second grade as I took my long morning walk to school. I managed to weave through the listless morning crowd and make it to my seat before the bell rang. I took out my number two pencils, marble notebook, and Ninja Turtles lunch box. I stacked my loose-leaf papers on my desk and braced myself for the worst as a figure walked into the room. I looked up and was pleasantly surprised. My new teacher did not even resemble Mrs. Noodleman at all. The new teacher even smiled when she looked at us. I started to ease up and pay attention to what this new teacher had to say. She announced to the class that her name was Ms.

Petite and that she was our new third grade teacher. Her voice was a sweet relief from the scratchy tone of Mrs. Noodleman. Ms. Petite had the deepest shade of blue in her eyes with bright blond hair to contrast them. She was thin and pretty; a gift considering Mrs. Noodleman's less than appealing semblance.

So with the introduction out of the way, Ms. Petite went on to teach the class about mathematics. I learned that one apple plus another apple equaled two apples. But the strange thing was, I could not apply that knowledge to numbers. I went through most of the third grade mathematics class counting apples. Despite that minor flaw, my knowledge was expanding in all directions. I learned that the world is covered mostly with water, the pilgrims came on a boat to America, and that Mississippi was a particularly difficult word to spell correctly. None of this business with SAT's, college applications, or GPA's ever crossed my mind. Life was good.

However, one day during the third grade, I found out how diseases travel through the human race. When the lunch bell rang at eleven-o-clock, I sprinted down to the cafeteria and took my place in the lunch line. It was Thursday which meant, according to my lunch schedule calendar, it was sloppy Joe Thursday. In every elementary school student's heart, Thursday was held near and dear. Due to the rise of childhood obesity, the school cut fatty foods a couple of years ago. Now we were subjected to "Veggie Burger Mondays" and "Whole Wheat Wednesdays".

However, on Thursday, globs of ground meat flowed abundantly from the ladle of Sloppy Joe himself.

When I finally arrived before the blessed spoon of Sloppy Joe, he suddenly sneezed on my lunch. I looked up at him and saw that he was in a terrible condition. His face seemed robbed of his convivial blush. His eyes looked as if it had receded into his skull. And his nose dripped of mysterious fluid that seemed to have invaded his nasal cavities. He apologized immediately and offered me a new plate, but I felt so bad for him that I accepted the diseased plate. Besides, the line behind me was growing fierce with hunger. I found my usual table and sat down with my chunky germ soup. I looked down on the plate, but the aroma of the seasoned beef was irresistible. I grabbed a spoon and shoveled hot sloppy joe into my mouth.

The next morning, I felt as if the whole earth was spinning wildly off its axis. My head felt hot, my chest hurt, and I could not stop coughing. My attempt to get myself out of bed was foiled by my weak knees and throbbing head. I mustered up enough strength to call out to my mother and tell her my condition. Of course, my mother thought I was deceiving her, so she just smiled at me and told me to get ready for school. I grumbled and shuffled my way to my room to dress myself and get my backpack. I went to the bathroom and glanced at the mirror. I looked pale, exhausted, and feeble, just like Sloppy Joe. I gave a big sigh and made my way to the front door.

As I left my house and headed towards the school, dizziness invaded my brain again. The trees seemed to melt away and the sidewalk seemed to stretch for eternity. Throughout this whole ordeal, I just told myself that I will be okay because my mother told me so. I took six confident strides in the direction of my school and everything went black. I woke up in my bed with sweat on my brow and a bag of ice on my head.

When my eyelids finally cracked open, I assumed that I was dead and in heaven. It was strange because heaven seemed noisier than advertised. It took my eyes a couple of minutes to regain focus, but when it did, I realized that I was in my room.

My mother was at my side with a glass of water and some Tylenol. She said that I had passed out on the sidewalk near our house and that she had run out and picked me up. As I laid there in my bed, I tried to trace the origin of my illness. I thought of everything that could have put me in this lamentable position. Finally, after eliminating every plausible explanation, I realized that Sloppy Joe's germs landed on my food and entered my body. I pictured all of the detestable germs running through my body, and my stomach suddenly felt unusually light. All the lights in the room seemed to amplify as all the shadows grew darker. Thankfully, the peculiar behavior of my body finally ceased when I doubled over and threw up on the side of my bed. I never desired sloppy joe ever again.

Now that I learned how illnesses were transmitted, I took extreme caution when I exposed myself to the germ infested world. I would not touch railings, share drinks, or even sit next to a sick person. When I needed to get out of the bathroom, I waited for another person to open the door so that I would not have to touch the doorknob. I could see the germs wriggling all around me and I could not accept the filth. The sloppy joe incident ran through my memory whenever I saw someone sneeze or cough. I carried a pack of disinfectant wipes and a bottle of Purell everywhere I went. I was made a slave to cleanliness and was trapped in a paranoid state of mind. As you can imagine, I did not play outside very often because of my fear of germs. I grew pale and thin due to the lack of sunlight and exercise and that made me a perfect target for schoolyard bullies.

It was five minutes until lunchtime and the anticipation for recess threatened to rupture within every young boy and girl. All attention was now fixed on the rusted analog clock on the wall as twenty-four minds simultaneously counted down the seconds. Even the teacher gave up her attempt to hold the students' attention and watched the clock. With every inch gained by the minute hand, eyes widened and bottoms shifted towards the edge of their seats. After five long minutes of urging and pleading, the clock's hand finally obeyed the students' request and signaled the start of lunch. The bell gloriously rang through the halls as herds of elementary school students barreled out from classrooms.

As I made my way out from my classroom, I was mowed down by a bulky shoulder. I fell to the tiled floor and turned around to face my aggressor. As soon as my eyes met his beady stare, I knew that I was in trouble. I had just gotten in the way of Jared, the enormous fourth grade bully. He loomed over me, blocking the sunlight with his frightening frame. He jabbed his fleshy arms towards my shirt collar and curled his stubby fingers around it. With a grip as firm as vice, he lifted me up to his face and screamed, "Hey, Pencil-Neck! You made me drop my sandwich!"

I looked over to the pile of meat and bread next to his size 6 sneakers and realized that I had indeed ruined his lunch. I quivered under his tight grip and braced myself for a barrage of angry fists. Right when I was fully prepared to take a punch to my stomach, the teacher rushed over and pried me loose from Jared's death-grip. As soon as my feet made contact with the tiled floor, I scrambled down the hallway and towards the cafeteria. I looked back at the classroom and once again met Jared's cold stare.

Once I entered the cafeteria, the familiar smell of cooked grease and packaged lunches soothed my troubled mind. I sat down with my friends and told them of my recent attack. My friends gasped as I weaved a tall tale about how I confidently knocked Jared's sandwich out of his hand and pummeled him to a pulp. I stretched the truth as far as I could. I stretched it until my story seemed outlandish and ridiculous, but I did not care. Jared was two floors above me, probably serving detention.

As I gave a playful bow to my friends' applause, I saw something that drained the blood from my face. With my head still down from the bow, I saw a pair of size 6 sneakers angry tapping its foot on the slick cafeteria floor. By the time I pulled my head back, I was sailing through the lunchroom air. I landed in a heaping plate of Tuesday's Tuna Fish Surprise about three feet from my table. I reached for my anti-bacterial wipes in my pocket and wiped my face clean from the tuna fish. When my vision returned, I swung my head back up and witnessed one of the most frightening scenes of my life.

Jared was charging towards me at full speed with a curled fist in one hand and a cafeteria tray in the other. Time seemed to slow down and Jared's rampage was the only image entering my now round eyes. I wondered if I was going to die; if Jared will actually punch me to death. Well, that was the last thought that ran through my mind because Jared was now inches away from my fragile frame. He hit me like a truck would hit a deer or how a foot would stomp an ant. Fists were colliding with my bones and feet were crashing into my stomach. Although the attack only lasted about fifteen seconds, I felt that I had been tortured for a lifetime. A janitor finally tore Jared's corpulent body away and escorted me to the nurse's office.

When I arrived at the nurse's office, everybody in the room gasped and stared. My nose was dripping with blood and bruises riddled my body. As I approached the head nurse, her assistant nurse ran to get gauze and anti-bacterial cream. The head nurse was paralyzed with astonishment and did nothing but stare at my dismal condition. After about a minute of inspection, she rose from her chair and took out a band-aid. She stuck the colorful band-aid on one of my wounds, stepped back to recheck her work, and sat back down in her chair. If I was not so battered, I would have laughed out loud.

How could a small strip of adhesive paper heal my bruises and cuts? Well at least the assistant nurses treated my injuries properly. They doused my cuts with hydrogen peroxide and mended my broken body. The nurses even gave me a Jolly Rancher on the way out of the office. As I limped out of the room and into the musty hallways, I realized that even a small third grader was not safe from the world's harm.

The rest of my third grade school year was fairly wonderful despite that one tussle with Jared. I made new friends and learned the all the necessary things a boy of the third grade needs. After meeting all the requirements to pass the third grade, the school dismissed the students and gave us two whole months of summer fun. Like every other summer, I spent my vacation in Long Island with my cousins. My parents would drop me and my sister off in Long Island for the entire summer. My cousins and I played in their large backyard until there was no more light in the sky. Some days, we would play Indians and Cowboys and other days we would play Cops an Robbers. But sometimes my aunt would take us to the amusement park for the entire day. I remember the first time I went to an amusement park. I remember the distinct smell of buttered popcorn looming through the air. I remember the ear-shattering screeches of roller coaster riders. The amusement park's charm wrapped around all my senses as I stood near the entrance, bewildered by the lights and sounds.

When I finished taking in the majesty of the amusement park, I followed my cousins to a long line of people. I did not understand what this line was for. Then, suddenly, a blur of intense screaming whipped above my head. I instantly turned around to see what that mysterious blur was. When I lifted my face to the sky, my gaze was met with a great tangle of twisted metal. I stammered, "W-We're going on th-that thing?"

My cousins turned around with a devilish grin and confirmed my nightmare. At that moment, I fled from the line and retreated back to where my aunt was standing. I buried my timorous face into my aunt's stomach, wishing that I had never come to such a perilous place.

But I could not eradicate this inner feeling of curiosity. So, after I calmed down, I released my face out from my aunt's stomach and watched my cousins pierce through the sky. With every sharp turn, my stomach seemed to turn with the cart. With every gravity-defying loop, my brain seemed to perform a back flip. The ride finally came to a halt, and I rushed over to my cousins to check if they were still alive. When I saw their faces, I realized that they could not have been more alive. They stumbled out from the walkway with disheveled hair and smiles ripped from ear to ear. The sight of my cousin's euphoria

The year is 1997, and I just came back from Public School 79 in Flushing, New York. The school was grand in size and seemed endless in capacity. The rooms were brightly colored and littered with decorations. I always enjoy my time at the school, but this time it was different. It was Halloween and as usual Mom did not get me a costume. She believed that Halloween was "for the devil and only evil children celebrated it". I begged and pleaded with all the fiber in my body for a costume and eventually she caved in and agreed to let me dress up. Fervent with elation, I started to choose what I would be. Would I be a scary zombie? Or a blood-curling werewolf? Maybe a ghoulish ghost?

No. I had to be a businessman. Of course, I did not know my embarrassing fate until the morning of Halloween. I woke up earlier than usual to put on my costume, but my excitement was met with a dull, over sized, 1980's afflicted flannel suit. I could see the insipidness dripping from the fabric. I could feel the tackiness with each thread and stitch.

For a moment, I simply looked back at this suit and then to my mother's face. My mother had this smile that only an immense accomplishment can muster. She nodded at me with a smile, a signal to try on the costume. I reluctantly put on the suit and tie while my mother ran to get her camera. My tiny, awkward frame was lost in a sea of itchy fabric. I went to school wearing the mediocre costume while my peers proudly strode down the hallways in their elaborate outfits. I did not even bother to go trick-or-treating in efforts to hide myself from my friends. Instead of venturing into the darkness for sweets, my family sat in the dark with all the lights off to discourage trick-or-treaters from knocking at our door.

I guess my mother felt sympathetic because when Halloween came around again in 1998, she let me and my sister dress up in more interesting costumes. I got to wear a Batman costume while my sister wore a Wonderwoman outfit. I paraded down the halls of my school, showing off the intricate details of my costume. When the school day was over, my sister and I visited my cousins in Bayside, Queens. However, when we arrived at their house, there was nobody in building. My mother found a note telling her that my cousins had a doctor's appointment. So, in full costume, my sister and I sat on the couch and waited for my cousins. While we were waiting, my sister had the brilliant idea of hiding underneath the coffee table and surprising my cousins. I agreed to the plan and crouched below the small wooden table. After a couple of minutes, we heard the door slam shut. That was our cue to pop out and give my cousins' a proper scare.

We emerged from under the table and made the most sound our little vocal chords could possible handle. We shook our arms in the air and sprung towards our cousins. My sister and I took off our masks and roared with laughter. We pried ourselves from our laughter to see our cousins' reaction to our prank. Unfortunately, our cousins did not enjoy the prank as much as my sister and I did. In fact, they were so shocked that they began to bawl uncontrollably. My aunt yelled at me and my sister for being so mean and confiscated our costumes. So much for the holiday spirit.

Every Christmas day, our family would get up early and go to the Christmas service at church. There were always hymns to be sung, prayers to be prayed, and greetings to be given. One Christmas morning, my sister and I left for the youth service at church. Supposedly, Santa Claus was scheduled to arrive at our chapel and distribute gifts to us. Although a good number of children firmly believed that Santa would show up, I had my doubts about the jolly man. If he was so nice, why would he only come once a year to give children presents? I just did not get it. I left the chapel and made my way upstairs to where the adults were having their service. Maybe my father would provide the answer to my questions. I scanned the immense room for my father's face but came up empty handed. I searched in every pew and balcony and still could not locate my father.

As I searched the upper floors, I saw a pile of clothes and a pair of shoes in the corner of the room. I approached the pile of garments and noticed that they were the exact same clothing that my father wore this morning.

How could this be? I quickly made a mental list which identified all the possible explanations of my father's missing clothing.

First, I hypothesized that my father turned invisible and therefore clothing would be unnecessary. Then, I suspected that my father was warming up too quickly in the densely packed chapel so he removed his clothing to cool off. After several absurd explanations of my father's abandoned clothing, I grew tired and decided to go back to the youth group chapel and wait for Santa Claus to arrive.

Well, I waited there in the chapel for this legendary man in red. I waited and waited until my patience grew as thin as wire. Suddenly a spot of red infiltrated my peripheral vision. I swung my head towards the figure and I was thoroughly shocked. It was him! He really did exist! I sprinted across the room to the gathering crowd of youngsters. I shoved my way through the screaming kids and got a good look at this beloved man.

Peculiar, Santa Claus wore the exact same glasses as my father. While I was observing his glasses, Santa reached out and picked me up from the crowd. He propped me up on his shoulders and asked me what I wanted. Strange, Santa Claus had the same scent as my father. Even before I could reveal my most wanted item, Santa pulled a Play Doh set out from his enormous bag of toys. Impossible, my father was the only one who knew I wanted a Play Doh set. Despite my suspicion, I quickly grabbed my gift out from his hands and let a grin sprawl itself across my face. When I looked back at Santa Claus's face, he gave me a wink and said, "Merry Christmas, David! You were a good boy this year. Have fun with your toy and remember to share with your sister."

After those words left his mouth I instantly knew who was behind the beard and costume. I could recognize that baritone voice from a mile away. It was my father and with a little help from a red suit and some stuffed pillows, he took on the role of Santa Claus. I gave my father a hug and thanked him for the present. After the service was over, I ran to my father's car and could not wait to expose him as Santa Claus. When I flung myself into the car and shut the door, I immediately accused my father of being Santa Claus. Words left my mouth at an unbelievable and almost indecipherable rate. However, my father calmly denied every accusation and claimed to have been with my mother the whole time. I could not believe it. As I dealt with the confusion, I saw my father with a suppressed grin on his face through the reflection of the rear-view mirror. What was he so happy about?

Our Thanksgivings were spent mostly in Long Island, New York, with my cousins. On Thanksgiving morning, our family jam into the car and endured a long trip to Long Island. When we got there, we cheerfully greeted our cousins and family members with hugs and handshakes. While everybody was greeting one another, I set out to explore the house. My cousins' house seemed gargantuan to me. It had three floors, three bathrooms, and an immense backyard. I was always jealous of their house because our house was only large as their garage. My cousins had swing sets, a basketball hoop, video games, large televisions, and every other imaginable distraction for a young child.

So while the adults chatted with other family members, my two cousins, my sister, and I played together. One Thanksgiving, we even made a play based on the origins of the holiday. I was a Native American rowing a boat, my cousins were the explorers who landed on Plymouth Rock, my sister was the captain of the ship, and my uncle played a turkey. After hours of practice and preparation, we took the living room as the stage and unleashed our masterpiece to the family. The play did not go exactly according to plan, but it did not matter. Everybody was laughing and having a good time together. I felt that the only place where I would not be judged was in the living room with my family. No matter how unskilled of an actor I was, my family still gave me a standing ovation. After some cheering and compliments, we all headed for the dining table to feast on the rewards of Thanksgiving.

My family consists of my father, my mother, my sister, and my grandmother. Of course I have other family members, but those four members were the most prevalent in my life. My father, Inkuk Yun (or Richard), is a very traditional and strict Korean man. He adheres to his sense of morals to an extreme length, usually causing a conflict in one way or another.

His tolerance for failure or inadequacy is extremely low. If I did not achieved nothing short of excellence, he would express his discontent very strongly. My father does not accept mediocrity or gray areas; he strives for the best and has raised me to do the same. However, many times during my childhood, my achievements have left my father disappointed and angered. During my years as a middle schooler to a freshman in high school, my grades have been dismally low. I dreaded the days when report cards returned and revealed the F's and D's. The first thing that rushed into my head as I saw my grades was the sound of my father's voice of anger. His voice sounded like God's if God was filled with rage and roaring at you from the heavens. I was so terrified by my father that I started to hide my faults in any way possible. When I got a bad grade, I would hide my report card and blame the postman for late deliveries. When I got into a fight in school, I would blame my opponent and claim complete innocence. His presence struck fear into my heart and drove me to extreme measures to avoid criticism.

However, my father was predictable and constant in his anger; my mother was not. Don't get me wrong; there were times in my life when my mother was the most loving specimen on the planet, but there were also times when my mother's ire burned me. My father was consistent and stable during his lectures and punishments, but my mother was incalculable and volatile. One minute she would be calm and quiet then suddenly become excited and full of anger. It's not that my mother was an angry tyrant all the time; it's just that when she was ill-tempered, I ran for cover.

There was a time in my childhood when I left my house without informing my parents and went out with my friend. I do not know what I was thinking, but I just stepped out of my door and followed my friend to the park. It was not out of discontent or rage, but simply out of pure childhood stupidity. In the park, my friend and I found an abandoned baseball bat and played baseball until it was pitch dark. On my way home, a police car pulled up next to me and asked me my name and address. As soon as I blurted out my name he insisted that I get in the car because my parents are looking for me.

As you can assume, the scene at my house was both dramatic and chaotic. There were at least five police cars lined up near my driveway with their lights and horns piercing through the neighborhood. After the cops left my street and all the commotion faded away, my mother grabbed the "punishment stick" and whipped the back of my calves. As she was striking me she declared, "I'm doing this because I love you!" Of course, at the time that was nonsense; how can such searing and skin breaking welts be outcomes of love? As I retreated back to my room I assured myself that I would understand the paradoxical nature of Korean-style punishment. I never did.

You may be wondering why I would portray my parents in such a dark and unfavorable light. As I was preparing to write this part of my autobiography, I earnestly tried to find a genuine moment in which my family shared a beautiful moment, together. I sat in my chair, straining to dig up such memories, but I became so frustrated that I gave up and went to sleep.

As I laid there in the dark, I could not help but feel disturbed that I could not recall any fond memories of my family. I felt cheated and scammed because I assumed that the ideal family was suppose to share every waking moment smiling and giving each other compliments. Families like the ones on Full House, Family Matters, 7th Heaven, etc., were all paragons for the ideal family.

However, I realize now that those families were concocted for entertaining the masses and not to reflect real families. The problem was not that my parents were inadequate, but that my expectations were unrealistic. I expected my father to conform to an unrealistic model of a father set by actors like Bob Saget. I yearned for the constant compliments and approval that Bob Saget gave on his show. Well, nobody can have Bob Saget as their father. Similarly, I wanted my mother to mirror the mothers on TV dramas with their kind words and unremitting love. In the end, I am thankful that my parents were not perfect because it shook me and made me realize that the relationship between expectations and reality is usually very distant.

Not to risk sounding like an ungrateful snob, I must talk about the sacrifices my parents made for my well-being. Both my mother and my father were born and raised in South Korea. My father lived the definition of sacrifice; he lived in poverty. One thing I envy most about my father is that he always follows through on his goals. Anybody can say that they will study hard to lift themselves out of poverty, but it takes an extraordinary person to follow through with unremitting diligence. My father placed top rank in every study in his class. From mathematics to history, my father studied until his body wore out. With vast knowledge and limitless potential, my father migrated to America to find opportunity and better life for his future children.

However, his immigrant status stifled his opportunities. The language barrier blocked him from the highest paying jobs that he so deserved. He was a lion pacing in a restrictive cage. My dad compromised his dreams and aspirations for higher knowledge to provide me with a comfortable life. I never had to go through starvation,

I never had to live in poverty. His hard, menial job was my life bread. My father continues to sacrifice himself to provide me with a comfortable present and an optimal future. He did not "invest" in my education. Investments produce profitable returns, and my father did not seek to profit from my education. My dad was more like the primary benefactor to my future. He traded his income for my elementary books. He exchanged his time for my tutor classes. He sacrificed his present for my future.

My mother was born in September 15, 1963, in South Korea. She lived a fairly comfortable life, but not an extravagant one. She was a tomboy when she was growing up in Korea. With her hair cut short and her tough jackets on her back, my mother was a strong and very independent young woman. She would often tell me stories of how tough she was back in her youthful days. My mother would pummel bullies to the ground, win arm wrestles against her father, and move heavy objects for her household.

Despite her remarkable toughness, she did not lack intelligence. She majored in foreign language and excelled in French and Spanish. My mother's dream as a young woman was to travel and learn all about different cultures. However, like my father, when she arrived in America, she had to give up her hopes and dreams of traveling around the world. Finding a steady job was difficult for my mother because she was an immigrant and a woman. Those two obstacles barred her from the top paying jobs in America. Although she came to this country with the American dream in mind, reality was that not everybody was eligible for limitless success.

Although my mother's potential was restrained by her immigrant status, she still worked hard to support me and my sister. There were days when my mother came home drained of all her energy. I could see the strain in face as she struggled to make her way across the living room. Despite her lassitude, she would never fail to greet me with a smile and a hug. After only fifteen minutes of rest, my mother marched out from her bed and cooked dinner. Her cooking was not the best in the world, but the fact that she poured all her energy and love into the food gave it an enticing aroma.

Right before the meal, our father said a prayer for all of us. I can still hear his low humble tone echoing through our small apartment building. After we ate dinner, my mother washed all the dishes and put back all the utensils. I would sometimes see my mother grab her back in pain and just sit on the kitchen floor for a while. That sight would always make me want to cry. I realized how much my mother was working to support our family. She was squeezing every drop of energy from her fragile body to keep our family from starving. It amazed me how far my mother pushed herself past her boundaries to keep me healthy and happy. It would be an atrocity not to thank my mother for her hard work. Thank you, mom.

I never felt that I had a best friend. That may sound sad, but I actually prefer it that way. Let me explain. A person always wants to show the best of themselves when they meet new people. However, if a person gets too comfortable with their friends, they start to show their true character. Anger, jealousy, indolence, whatever it may be, they all show up when a person is too comfortable around their peers. Why not avoid all those unpleasant characteristics? But that's not to say that the people around me are unpleasant; they are all wonderful people. What I am saying is that I am a casual friend. General purpose; that's what it is. That is what I am. Sure, I have a few light friends and some good companions, but no one I cannot live without.

The migration from New York to New Jersey was an immense change in my life. I always imagine how different I would have been if I had remained in New York. My home in New York was located right in front of a busy street in Queens. The streets were always invested with loud cars and even louder drivers. The lights never went out either. Our little one floor apartment was enveloped by neon lights and rumbling engines. When we finally moved to Ridgewood, New Jersey, it was dead quiet. The tall flickering buildings were replaced by towering oak trees. The incessant noise of traffic was replaced by the occasional chirp of birds and crickets. I scanned the new suburban neighborhood, with its identical houses and cookie cutter lawns, and realized that I was enclosed by the elderly. At night I lay on my bed, praying for an onslaught of honking cars to parade through the streets, so I can fall asleep.

It was the summer of 2005, and I had just finished 7th grade. Fresh from the perils of the middle school, I was ready for a summer of indolence and relaxation. I remember the bell screeching its last cry as three-o-clock finally blinked onto the clock's display. I darted out from the stuffy classroom and into the hallways filled with jubilation. Paper planes soared through the air, old homework fell into garbage cans, and eager children raced down the hall. I eventually navigated myself through the thick throng of students and left the school to go home. When my mother arrived, she looked particularly excited. She rolled down the window and exclaimed, "Hey! We're going to Korea!" and gave me a huge grin.

I had mixed feelings about going to Korea. First off, I lost most of my Korean language skills during my years as an American student. Secondly, I had a fear of traveling in planes. Sure they all claim that the plane is safe and dependable, but who can guarantee that a bolt does not come loose or an engine does not malfunction? On the other hand, I was excited to finally visit the place where my culture was born. I imagined a land of rural fields and rustic lifestyle.

When I arrived in Seoul, Korea, my previously held perception was shattered. I could not spot a grassy plain for miles. It seemed as if New York City had been drained of all its American city goers and replaced with Korean people. The city was saturated with lights, noise, and smoke. The bustling city swallowed me whole, and I immersed myself in the dense crowd. I felt like I belonged in this city as I looked around to see millions of Koreans – just like me.

I followed my mother and my sister through the winding streets of Korea to my mother's old house. As we left the roaring city, suddenly the streets turned to cobblestones, the skyscrapers melted down to modest apartments, and the grit and grime of the city were taken over by miles of sand and ocean. After walking through the sweltering heat for hours, we finally reached our destination.

I looked through a shoddy black gate to see an apartment at a dead end alley. Although the house seemed ominous to me, my mother was more than eager to climb those rickety stairs to her former home. When we entered the house, we were greeted with shouts of joy and surprise. A fragile old woman waddled quickly towards us with a smile and open arms. My mother seemed to fit perfectly into the arms of my grandmother. The woman had wrinkles running all over her face like a cracked piece of pottery.

www.ingramcontent.com/pod-product-compliance
Lightning Source LLC
Chambersburg PA
CBHW032003080426
42735CB00007B/498